GHOSTS OF OLD MUNCIE

CHRIS FLOOK

Published by Haunted America
A Division of The History Press
Charleston, SC
www.historypress.com

First published 2024

Manufactured in the United States

ISBN 9781467157872

Library of Congress Control Number: 2024936787

Notice: The information in this book is true and complete to the best of our knowledge. It is offered without guarantee on the part of the author or The History Press. The author and The History Press disclaim all liability in connection with the use of this book.

Thomas Kirby, late nineteenth century.
Courtesy of Ball State University Libraries'
Bracken Archive and Special Collections.

This book is dedicated to the memory of Mike Mavis, a good friend and fellow public historian. Mike told me a ghost story once at the Fickle Peach about Thomas Kirby, an early Muncietown settler. Mike claimed that Kirby's ghost delighted in rolling his head down the stairs out at the old estate on East Jackson. Every time I drive by the Kirby House now—the grand 1839 manor still stands—I can't help but remember Mike gleefully pounding his fists on the table, mimicking the sound of a head rolling down stairs.

CONTENTS

ACKNOWLEDGEMENTS

Research for this book was only possible because of the expansive archives and collections available at the Delaware County Historical Society, Ball State University Libraries' Bracken Archive and Special Collections, Muncie Public Library, Minnetrista Museum and Gardens and the Yorktown–Mount Pleasant Historical Alliance. I'm blessed to live in a community with so many wonderfully rich repositories of history. I'm also grateful for the ease of online research at Newspapers.com, Ancestry.com, Hoosier State Chronicles, Library of Congress and the Internet Archive.

I'd like to especially recognize Becky Marangelli, archives specialist at Ball State's Bracken Library. She was instrumental in providing a dozen or so high-resolution images for this book. Local historian Jeff Koenker also lent a few from his personal collection, including a rare trolley photo. I deeply appreciate Mr. Koenker's support and his tireless work in preserving Delaware County's history.

I'm also thankful for John Rodrigue, acquisitions editor at The History Press. This is my fourth book with the publisher and third working with Mr. Rodrigue. He's guided me successfully through each and advocates for my ideas.

I'm also indebted to my mother, Kathie Flook. She provided feedback on early drafts and wrote the short stories for the prologue. Mom understands how good history is written, and I trust her judgment. I'm also thankful for my partner Kourtney's unending support while writing this book. She helps me carve space every day to write.

Most importantly, this book is only possible because of thousands of reporters, photographers, editors, cartoonists, writers, managers, sales staff, typesetters, essayists, interviewers, delivery persons and printers of Muncie's newspapers. For nearly two centuries, local papers chronicled Muncie and Delaware County daily life in detail. Without newspapers, Muncie wouldn't have much of a recorded history.

PROLOGUE

SOUTHSIDE HAUNTINGS

S oon after I began research for this book, I realized that there wasn't a realistic way to write about *every* ghost story and haunted house in Delaware County. During the year it took for me to write this, I heard dozens of uncanny tales about places like Muncie Civic Theater, the Delaware County Courthouse, Bracken Library, the Patterson Building, Cornerstone Center for the Arts, Carnegie Library, my own home in Kenmore and a Muncie west side apartment complex.

Lots of people, as it turns out, have ghost stories to share. To document every local haunting would require thousands of hours of interviews, hundreds of pages of text and a lifetime of research. I'm not sure such a work is even possible.

Nonetheless, *many* supernatural stories are set in and about Muncie and Delaware County. Just ask your friends and neighbors sincerely: "Have you ever seen a ghost?" You may even have a story yourself—a strange personal experience perhaps or maybe a tale passed down from relatives. My family members have several.

I asked my mother, Kathleen (Farr) Flook, to write three of them for this prologue. All are set in Muncie's Southside neighborhoods. In the 1940s, Mom and her family lived along Hackley Street, a few blocks south of Heekin Park. The Farrs moved across Madison to Congerville in 1955 and lived on Mulberry Street.

GRANDMA'S WARNING

By Kathleen Farr

I was about two, playing on the living room floor with my toys. Mom was in the basement doing laundry. She had one of those old wringer-type washers that made the chore labor-intensive.

Dad always left early for work because he was a contractor at Kirby Wood. He often had to travel distances for jobs. Maybe that particular morning he forgot to latch the front screen door. I was never allowed to go out of it by myself, yet I managed somehow to make it into the front yard. We lived on Hackley Street. It was busy with traffic even back then in the late '40s.

In the basement, a few minutes later, my mother was putting wet laundry through the wringer when she heard a familiar voice. She stopped and looked up. It sounded close by—a loud, agitated voice. She recognized it immediately as belonging to her mother, Dillie, who had died five years earlier.

"Mother?" she said hesitantly.

The voice shouted back, "Go now! Your baby is in the street. Hurry!"

Dropping our wet laundry, Mother ran up the stairs, through the kitchen and out the front door. There I was, standing at the edge of Hackley, ready to step into traffic. She swooped me up and ran into the house crying.

My mother was not a fanciful person and did not lie. If she said this happened, it did.

A GHOST IN THE CONGERVILLE HOUSE

By Kathleen Farr

It was summer. My sister and I were six and nine, playing house on the front porch. Mom was finishing the hems for our new bedroom window curtains. We had the middle room upstairs, and Dad had just re-wallpapered it. We were excited to move in. The room even had new rugs and bedspreads.

The front was open, with just the screen door closed. Mom was sewing in a rocking chair upstairs in our room. She could hear us playing on the porch, and we could hear her through the screen.

As she bent over her work, she suddenly sensed, rather than saw, something in the upstairs hall that passed the bedroom door.

The Farrs' Congerville house on Mulberry, circa 1955. *Courtesy of Kathleen Farr.*

Mom sprang to look. At the hallway's end, she saw the back of a strange woman who wore an old-fashioned lavender print dress with a white pinafore and high-top shoes. Her hair was swept up to the crown of her head.

The lady stood motionless in front of the closed door to Mom and Dad's bedroom. As Mom walked into the hall to look more closely, the mysterious woman vanished.

After investigating, she could not find anyone or anything amiss. Someone leaving the house would have had to pass Mom to get out downstairs.

My mother sat down and resumed her sewing, thinking she just imagined it all. She finished her work about the time we called up asking for lunch. She promised to come down soon and set her sewing aside on my sister's bed.

As she turned to leave, the strange lady reappeared and passed the door again but went in the opposite direction. She stopped at a linen closet and disappeared.

I overheard Mom telling Dad this story later. I asked her to tell me what had happened, and she did, but only on the condition that I not tell my sister, Pat, who was still very susceptible to nightmares. But the story didn't scare me.

Mom thought maybe it was someone who used to live in our house. She had grown up in the same neighborhood and knew all the families in Congerville.

THE LADY IN WHITE

By Kathleen Farr

Dad's family was very superstitious. We were not allowed to open an umbrella in the house or leave a chair rocking. He also once told us that a lady in white would come visit the bedside of a dying family member. He said this as matter-of-factly, as if he had told us it was raining outside.

One day in November 1979, I went over to take Dad to the doctor. He had been sick for a while but seemed to be on the mend. Mom and my sister, Pat, were both working, so I offered to drive him. It was cold and rainy out. I was about three months' pregnant and not feeling well.

Dad seemed down during the appointment, but the doctor was pleased with his progress. I took him home and we sat at the kitchen table to talk.

Eventually I got up to go and gave him a kiss goodbye, promising to bring my little girl the next time to see him. He still looked sad. I patted his shoulder and told him he was getting better. He shook his head no.

"I've seen her," he said.

I understood right away what he meant and left very troubled. Later that night, I got the call that Dad died in his sleep.

A white lady visiting a dying person in 1896, from the book *Ghostly Tales*. *Courtesy of the British Library*.

INTRODUCTION

In the spring of 1900, a ghost began haunting Wysor's Grand Opera House at the southwest corner of Jackson and Mulberry Streets. The *Muncie Morning Star* reported on March 31 that "strange noises have been heard at night and explanations are wanting."[1] Theater manager Harry Wysor claimed that "he had frequently heard the noises but could not explain them."

The day before, Muncie police captain Curtis Turner investigated the ghostly sounds with Wysor's security guard Charles Heffner. The cops searched the theater top to bottom but couldn't find a source or anything amiss. Then suddenly, according to Heffner, they were standing on stage and heard a loud "knock, very distinct, followed by others. Then a crash like that of a pile of furniture falling was heard, and in a few seconds, [the] sound like that of gravel falling on the roof."

Heffner made a point to tell the reporter, "I do not believe in ghosts or spirits." Captain Turner concurred but said that the sounds were still "mysterious and made him feel uncomfortable." Neither cop found what produced the uncanny racket.

Wysor's stagehands believed that the noises came from the ghost of James Linville, a former employee. Linville worked at the theater for a few years after it opened in 1892. He served first as a stagehand and later in advertising as a "bill poster." Sadly, his life was cut short because of tuberculosis. Linville died in 1898 and was buried at Beech Grove Cemetery. As his health failed and death loomed, he supposedly told fellow stagehands that "he would return, if possible, and visit them."

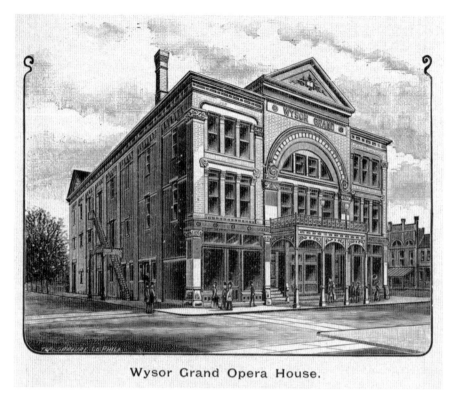

Wysor Grand Opera House.

Etching of the Wysor Grand Opera House in 1893. *Courtesy of the Delaware County Historical Society.*

It's unclear in the historical record when Linville's spirit stopped haunting Wysor's Grand. The last mention of it occurred in the *Herald* on April 2, 1900: "The ghost at the Wysor Grand has not been captured."[2] Today, there's nothing left of the theater for Linville's ghost to haunt. Wysor's Grand opera, vaudeville and movie house was razed in 1963 to make way for a parking lot.

As the stories in this book demonstrate, Muncie and Delaware County's ghosts need *places* to haunt. More precisely, Munsonians are haunted at *someplace*. A parking lot is a *noplace*—what respectable ghost wants to haunt a half acre of cracked asphalt and pungent Bradford pears?

Ghosts haunt people where they live, work and travel—houses and farms, neighborhoods and schools, forests and wetlands, old bridges and turnpikes, hotels, office buildings, stores, parks and factories. Any *place* we find people, we may catch glimpses of ghosts that haunt them.

The stories in this book are just that, glimpses of ghosts that haunted real living people in Muncie and Delaware County. As it turns out, the historical record yields dozens of uncanny tales. Some are long with many details, while others are nothing more than spooky little anecdotes. Although I suspect that most readers are familiar with this book's settings, I provided ample historical context so that each tale remains accessible to all, even nonlocals.

All readers should be aware that several chapters mention suicide and contain descriptions of self-harm. In no case do I exploit someone's demise by sensationalizing their manner of death, but historically suicide is part of several stories. Readers sensitive to such experiences should avoid chapters 1, 4, 5, 7, 9 and 11. I only include information if it's relevant to the story, but some of what follows includes detail.

Readers should also note that *Ghosts of Old Muncie* is a work of history and not folklore. Even though this book addresses the supernatural, all stories contained herein are rooted in local historical records. I thoroughly annotated everything and provided references to all source material for those interested in learning more.

Most of this book's history comes from local newspapers published in the late nineteenth and early twentieth centuries. I've added direct quotes

Otto Sellers's photo at the intersection of Mulberry and Jackson, looking south. Wysor Grand is on the right. *Courtesy of the Delaware County Historical Society, Mike Mavis Collection.*

A photo of a ghost, circa 1899. *Courtesy of Wikimedia Commons.*

throughout, mostly because I just like the language reporters used during this era. However, I didn't want to overburden readers by writing "the *Muncie Morning Star* reported that" a thousand times over. Instead, I opted for endnotes and worked the citations directly into the text.

I found many photos in Muncie archives to help tell these stories. Sadly, I didn't find any local historical photographs of ghosts. I did include nonlocal contemporary images of hauntings and spirits, along with spooky artwork from the relevant era. I hope these images provide readers with a sense of how our forebears imagined the uncanny when they encountered it.

I also didn't ask in this book or care to know if ghosts actually exist. To my mind, the question is irrelevant and, frankly, totally absurd. The people in these stories saw ghosts and were haunted by them. That's all that mattered to me.

Some hauntings were later revealed as elaborate pranks, while others never got an official explanation. In a few cases, some Munsonians conjured ghosts to terrorize and entertain one another. More often than not, apparitions became the form that grief, regret and fear manifested into during times of uncertainty. Occasionally, hauntings served as paranormal simplifications for phenomena that didn't seem to have any rational explanation.

Sometimes, though, Munsonians saw and heard very strange things they simply couldn't explain.

CHAPTER 1

A HAUNTED DELAWARE COUNTY

One thing is certain for me after researching and writing this book: Muncie and Delaware County are haunted places. In the chapters that follow, you'll read strange tales of supernatural apparitions, ghostly encounters, cyclical phantoms, haunted houses and a mysterious Woman in Black. For these stories, there was enough information in historical records to write whole chapters exploring the hauntings in detail, their settings and the people involved.

However, I also found several random but short references of ghostly encounters in Muncie's newspapers—one-off little nuggets of the uncanny. There isn't much to these paranormal incidents, but they do serve as anecdotal evidence suggesting that the dead have long been active in the community.

For example, the *Muncie Daily News* reported without any concern on September 23, 1882, that "Nat Lockwood saw a ghost."[3] That's all there is—there's no follow-up or any other context. It was one of several news blurbs in that day's edition, printed alongside such banality as "Mrs. Web Richey is in the city to-day" and "Mr. Woods' new barn on West Main street has been painted."[4]

"Nat Lockwood saw a ghost" might have been an inside joke or a reference to something entirely nonsupernatural. It's also possible that the historical person of Nat Lockwood really saw a ghost. Lockwood was a harness maker in Muncie at the time and worked at Husted, Wachtell and Company on East Main.[5] A talented musician, he traveled often with circuses, which is

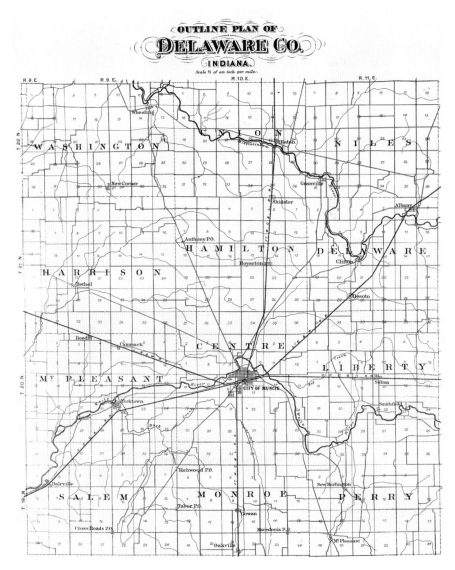

Above: Map of Delaware County as it appeared in 1881. From Thomas Helm's *History of Delaware County* (1881). *Courtesy of the Delaware County Historical Society.*

Opposite: Eleazor Coffeen's 1863 addition to Muncie, known commonly as "Coffin Town." *Courtesy of Delaware County, Indiana's Office of Information and GIS Services.*

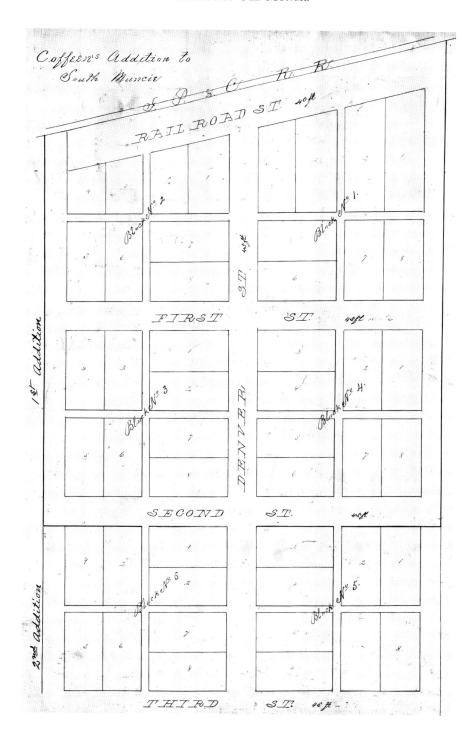

how he ended up in Muncie. He later moved to Frankfort, Indiana, and became a postal worker.[6] Perhaps Frankfort was less haunted.

Most accounts in this chapter happened in the late nineteenth and early twentieth centuries. Although some hauntings were explained rationally by reporters writing them, others weren't. What follows are spooky tidbits of history, marooned in time without much context or resolution.

A good example is a short blurb printed in the February 20, 1880 edition of the *Muncie Daily Times* about a haunted house on Muncie's near southside. In the "City Items" section, tucked between snippets about Reverend Clark Skinner's visit to Anderson and the theft of Moses McConnell's sawhorses, a reporter wrote that "there is a house in Coffeentown that is regarded by the superstitious, as being haunted, as strange sounds are heard both night and day. The house is at present unoccupied."[7]

Coffeentown—nicknamed, appropriately, at the time as "Coffintown"— was the informal name given to a south Muncie residential development along Madison Street. The neighborhood was platted in 1863 by a settler named Eleazer Coffeen. Coffeentown was bounded by the Bee Line (CSX) tracks north, Vine Street east, Second Street south and Madison Street west.

A decade later, in the summer of 1890, a poltergeist began terrorizing Fred Besser's farmhouse northeast of Muncie. The *Muncie Daily News* reported that "for the last week at very uncertain intervals, there has been a most mysterious stoning of his house, breaking windows and otherwise damaging things." Besser and fellow farmers kept a lookout but never saw the ghost, despite the "dirty work [having] appeared several times in broad daylight."[8]

Besser lived northeast of old Muncie in what is now Whitely Neighborhood. For many years, his estate was known as Smell Farm, so named in honor of Besser's late father-in-law and the farm's previous owner, Michael Smell.

By early August, rumors had begun circulating around northeast Center Township regarding the strange occurrences happening out on Smell Farm. The *Times* wrote on August 4 that "residents in the vicinity of the old Smell homestead, two miles northeast of the city, were badly frightened because of the unaccountable actions of an invisible stone throwing ghost." Besser and neighbors search but "failed to reveal any one as being the guilty person, and the family with others have concluded the house is doomed by a naughty ghost."

The next morning, the *News* dismissed the *Times*' story as township hogwash. "The people in that locality do not believe it" but instead were convinced "that it is some unprincipled fiend who has a spite at Besser."[9]

Left: Eleazor Coffeen, founder of Muncie's Coffintown "suburb." Engraving is from Thomas Helm's *History of Delaware County* (1881). *Courtesy of the Delaware County Historical Society.*

Below: The Michael Smell farm in Center Township as it appeared in the 1887 *Atlas of Delaware County*. Today, the farm is in the northwest section of Whitely, where Streeter meets Dr. MLK Jr. Boulevard. *Courtesy of the Delaware County Historical Society.*

Thankfully, the invisible rock thrower had "let up in the matter for a couple of days, and it is hoped that his 'ghostship' has seen the error of his ways."[10]

Three years later in May 1893, James Ellison blamed a ghost when his wife left him after a brief five-month marriage. Ida Winget married James the previous December, not long after her first husband died. Ellison believed that "since her last marriage she has often asserted that her former husband's spirit frequently haunts her as a punishment for breaking her promise" to not remarry.[11] Ida returned a few days later to collect her things, and the couple divorced. She later moved to Montpelier, Indiana, and died in 1934. She never remarried.[12]

About one month later, an unnamed squirrel hunter encountered a ghost east of Muncie at an old cabin across the White River from Muncie Waterworks. The *Muncie Daily Herald* wrote that a young hunter in the area witnessed the apparition one recent afternoon. At about 5:00 p.m., he fell asleep near the cabin under a tree. As the sun set, the huntsman abruptly woke and "was horrified to see the dim outlines of a figure in the doorway of the cabin. The young man's teeth chattered and his knees smote together."[13]

A grieving widow is haunted by her former husband lost at sea, circa 1903. Arthur Keller. *Courtesy of the Library of Congress.*

' THERE APPEARED, ALSO, THE DIM OUTLINE OF A

A woodcutting of a ghostly visitor in 1869 by the artist Charles Bush. *Courtesy of the New York Public Library Digital Collections.*

Terrified, he closed his eyes to shut out the creepy scene. When he opened them again, the phantom came at him. "All at once," the *Herald* exclaimed, "his courage returned and placing his shotgun against his shoulder, fired two loads of shot at the specter."[14] When the smoke cleared, the ghost was gone.

The *Herald* mused that the phantom was the vengeful spirit of a murdered peddler who had died in the cabin. One day in the early 1870s, "Two peddlers called at various houses in this city in an endeavor to sell their wares." One did well and the other didn't. A few days later "a peddler's empty pack similar to the one used by the fellow who had sold all his goods was found in the cabin covered in blood."[15] The *Herald* concluded that it is "now supposed that the young sportsman saw the ghost of the murdered peddler."[16]

It wasn't just squirrel hunters who saw ghosts—professional Munsonians did too. A police officer by the name of George Ball (no relation to the glass Ball brothers) routinely encountered a ghost at headquarters in downtown Muncie. Officer Ball often worked the night shift and bunked at the station. He had "frequently been aroused from deep slumber by mysterious rappings and noises which seemed to emanate from the northwest corner of the room in which police court is held."[17]

The Muncie Police Department was leasing the old *Muncie Daily Times* building at the corner of Walnut and Washington as its headquarters in 1893. *Herald* writers believed that the building was "visited in the dead of

Opposite: Muncie Police Department in 1895. *Courtesy of Ball State University Libraries' Bracken Archive and Special Collections.*

Above: *Harper's* illustration of a ghost haunting a man in 1894. Arthur Frost. *Courtesy of the Library of Congress.*

Muncie Times employees in 1893. *Courtesy of Ball State University Libraries' Bracken Archive and Special Collections.*

night by a ghostly visitor." MPD patrolmen working the graveyard shift, according to the *Herald*, were routinely beset "by the ghost of a tramp printer named Schumm."[18]

Several years prior, "Schumm called at the *Times* office, situated in the rooms now occupied by headquarters." With an extensive background in typesetting, Schumm asked for work and was given a job at a desk on the second floor "in the northwest corner of the room and worked steadily for a week." Come Saturday, he drew his pay and left. The next morning, his "headless body was found lying near the Big Four railroad between Winchester and this city."

The *Herald* was misremembering a genuinely tragic incident from 1890. A man by the name of William "John" Shumm had died of suicide that October. Upon learning of his death, the *Times* wrote that Shumm had worked for the newspaper off and on for about a year. He was an "excellent workman, was prompt, careful and industrious." His job was to set the paper's page plates for printers. He quit abruptly two months later after setting a story about a murder. It upset him, or as he put it, such things "followed him."

Hailing from Rush County, Shumm had served in the Union army during the Civil War, achieving the rank of corporal. He later married and had six children. His mental health suffered greatly after the war, as all contemporary sources indicated. Like most places at the time, Muncie had limited options to help someone in such distress.

TIMES BUILDING, MUNCIE, IND.

The old *Muncie Daily Times* building. Engraving is from Thomas Helm's *History of Delaware County* (1881). *Courtesy of the Delaware County Historical Society.*

In late September 1890, the *Times* needed extra help, and Shumm was called back to work. He performed his duties as before, but only for a week. He was found dead along the Big Four tracks on the morning of October 8, having stepped in front of a speeding eastbound train out of Muncie. The *Times* lamented that Shumm's "family and friends have the heartfelt sympathy of the entire community."[19]

The next day, the *Daily News* reflected that Shumm "started in life under favorable circumstances and as he was gifted with more than ordinary intelligence…[he] would have succeeded, but haunted by that awful phantom of his mind, he was wrecked in body and his life was ended."[20]

The village of Smithfield lies not far from where Shumm was found. As one of Delaware County's oldest communities, Smithfield grew initially as a

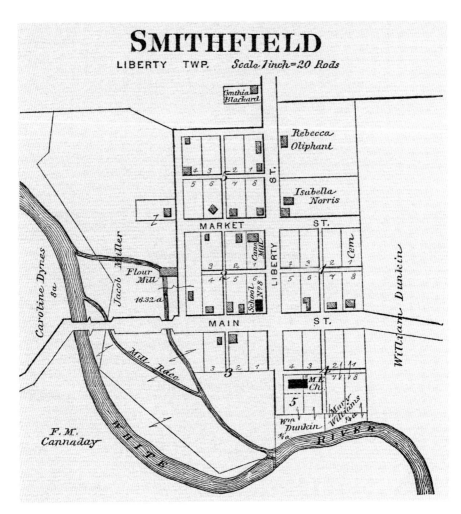

A map of Smithfield from the 1887 *Atlas of Delaware County. Courtesy of the Delaware County Historical Society.*

mill town and then expanded rapidly during the Indiana Gas and Oil Boom when oil was found beneath Liberty Township. Smithfielders witnessed ghosts at least twice by the end of the nineteenth century. On November 25, 1897, the *Daily Herald* reported that "some people of this place declared they saw a ghost Monday night."[21]

Two years later, the *Daily Times* reported that another "ghost is said to be stalking about the village of Smithfield, a few miles east of Muncie." Township farmers and residents "of Selma and Smithfield have been watching for it."[22]

In January 1899, the ghost of Lawrence Fritch began haunting the Albany Glass Factory. Fritch, a talented and well-known east-central Indiana glassmaker, had died of suicide earlier that month. The *Times* reported that "the spook goes about rattling the blow pipes and doing other things to scare the gathering boys." Fritch's replacement was Frank Lilly, who heard the "ghostly visitant as it talks through the funnel."[23]

In mid-October 1903, a bicycle thief named Elbert Taylor was haunted by *something* during his brief stay at the Delaware County Jail. The fourteen-year-old Taylor was arrested for stealing Glenn Forbis and Isaac Wagoner's bikes.[24]

The next morning, the *Times* reported that Taylor "was scared half to death last night in the jail and nothing can be said or done that will convince him that the cell in which he slept is not haunted." Taylor swore that "he saw a ghost not once, but many times."[25]

The *Times* leaned into the story:

> *Taylor was placed in a cell where a man once died and the other prisoners kept telling him horrible tales about the place. This morning Taylor said the ghost of the dead man kept him awake all night but he would not have cared for that but the spook insisted on pulling the covers off him every few minutes.*[26]

Both the sheriff and fellow jailbirds laughed it off, but young Taylor "is firm in the belief that the shade of the departed man came to haunt him."[27] He later pleaded guilty and "was let go under suspended sentence."[28]

There's a strange follow-up to this story. Two days later, the *Times* published a curious front-page article with a bold title: "Criminals Fear Supernatural."[29] The story featured an interview with Delaware County sheriff Orlando Swain. The sheriff made clear his thoughts about criminals and what haunted them:

> *There is no class of people in the world more superstitious than a hardened criminal. Anything apparently supernatural will cause him to go into spasms and a genuine crazy man will make the jail a place of horror. Let a man who is demented be placed in the jail and start to rave and there is not a man but will climb the bars or go to other extremes to get away.*[30]

Swain concluded, "No matter how hardened he be, a man who can commit murder and not have a qualm of conscience, when confronted

A ghost haunting a jail in Ida White's 1915 book, *Spirits Do Return. Courtesy of the Library of Congress.*

with what he imagines is a ghost, will be as meek as a lamb and will quake in fear."[31]

Four years later, in November 1907, a carpenter by the name of James Battles "thought he saw ghosts and other things" about his house on South Elm Street. On the evening of November 19, neighbors called police to

Stereographs were common in the late nineteenth century, as was spirit photography. Melander and Brother. *Courtesy of the Library of Congress.*

report Battles "shooting through the windows of his own home with a shotgun." The troubled carpenter had shot out all his windows along with one of his neighbor's.[32]

The *Muncie Evening Press* reported that Battles "insisted on quoting scripture and informing the police that he had been warned of their coming and was prepared to kill them." Battles saw "ghosts coming into his house yesterday. He barricaded himself and shot at random."[33] Luckily his arrest ended without violence.

Edward Wilson was another haunted soul in Muncie. On April 4, 1909, Wilson attempted suicide by drinking laudanum to relieve "his uncanny torture of mind." The eighteen-year-old Wilson worked at the Whiteley Malleable factory west of McCulloch Park. After Wilson downed an opium tincture, relatives found him unconscious in the family's barn. Soon-to-be mayor Dr. Rollin Havilla Bunch was called to administer care. Doc Bunch rendered "immediate medical aid" and saved the young man's life.[34]

Edward was distraught over a recent fight with family members. The Wilsons were mourning their father Emanuel's recent death. The elder Wilson had died of suicide two years before, leaving Edward and his brother, three sisters and their mother in a financial bind. The *Muncie Morning Star* reported that at night, "when young Wilson lies down to slumber, he seems to think the corpse of his dead father hovers about his bedside and tries to communicate with him."[35]

Wilson told Muncie police chief Van Benbo that "his father's spirit manifests itself to him in a most uncanny manner, as it comes to him and

Elliott Hall, circa 1938. *Courtesy of Ball State University Libraries' Bracken Archive and Special Collections.*

Beneficence on the campus of Ball State University. *Courtesy of the Delaware County Historical Society, Mike Mavis Collection.*

places its deathly cold hand on his brow and cheeks, bringing indescribable torture to his morbid mind."[36] Wilson was released to the care of his mother.

Reports of local hauntings and ghostly encounters mostly disappeared from local newspapers by World War I. But that's not to say ghost stories vanished entirely in Muncie and Delaware County in the twentieth century—we just need to look deeper to find them.

In *The Other Side of Middletown*, the 2004 seminal book about Muncie's African American history, the authors write about a ghost named "Black Annie" that haunted Willard Street in the twentieth century. The authors cite a story from a Munsonian named Renzie Abram who grew up hearing about Black Annie from a preacher named Elder Hosea Barnes. Abram "recalled Elder Barnes telling the congregation about the trees that hung low on Willard Street. They would summon 'Black Annie' to come and get you if you didn't run fast enough."[37]

During a research session for *The Other Side of Middletown*, many Black Munsonians remembered various iterations of the Black Annie story. Everyone seemed to have a tale to share. "One person said it was a story told by parents to encourage kids to come in before dark."[38]

In the latter half of the twentieth century, a ghost legend began circulating among college students about a haunting at Elliott Hall, a dorm on Ball State University's campus. The story was recounted by reporter Keith Roysdon just before Halloween in 1986. Roysdon wrote that "legend has it that William Shamberg returned to the university following the war. He had been disfigured and disabled in battle and was shunned by his fellow students. Following Christmas break—specifically on Jan. 26, 1947— Shamberg climbed the marble steps to the library on Elliott's north end. There he took his own life."[39]

The story is still occasionally shared around campus and appears now and then in student publications. One of the first printings was on January 16, 1986, when Diane Goudy wrote an article about Elliott Hall in the *Ball State Daily News*: "According to tradition, occasionally on cold and windy nights, Schamberg's ghost stalks the upper floor of the hall taunting residents with fleeting appearances and rattling within the walls."[40]

There's no truth to the story. No one named Shamberg (or Schamberg) died that day, according to county death records, nor did a "William Shamberg" ever attend Ball State. Roysdon checked, and "local veterans services make no mention of a William Shamberg serving in World War II."[41]

Elliott Hall isn't the only haunted building on Ball State's campus. Someone under the screen name "popeguilty" wrote a ghost story on the popular Reddit website about a haunting in Bracken Library. Popeguilty was studying late one evening on the fifth floor.[42] They headed for a bathroom on a study break but couldn't get the door open. "I gave it a good, hard shove, thinking that the door was jammed, and the door swung open slightly—*and then slammed shut, feeling for all the world as if someone was pushing on the other side of the door.*"[43] Eventually, the door gave way and the student entered.

Frightened and "weirded out," they noticed a "sourceless shadow on the ground in front of one of the urinals. As I watched, it moved down the row of urinals before vanishing under a stall door." A scratchy voice said, "Mine!" Terrified, the student ran out of Bracken, never to return.

Online sources of varying credibility have trafficked Muncie ghost stories for years. An old Angelfire.com site archives two short tales of Muncie hauntings, including at an apartment on West Sixth Street where "weird occurrences like past tenants waking up and having some sort of oil dumped on them."[44] The other is of a now demolished haunted restaurant called Carter's Skyline. The ghost of the old owner haunted the place by turning "lights on and off. Also, footsteps can be heard at night."[45]

Finally, lest you assume that ghosts were a thing of previous centuries, a man was arrested on April 8, 2020, after breaking into Wes-Del High School, northwest of Muncie near Gaston.[46] The world was on edge that April due to the onslaught of the COVID-19 pandemic. When the school custodian found the trespasser, the man raised his hands and said, "Don't mean you any harm....I was being chased by a ghost."[47]

CHAPTER 2

THE WOMAN IN BLACK

A Union Traction trolley made its way up Walnut Street in the evening of Saturday, September 28, 1907. The streetcar was on its last run of the day, headed into downtown from Muncie's southside Congerville suburb. As the car bounded north, the "motorman spied a woman standing close to the rails,"[48] obscured partially in shadow. The conductor later told a reporter that she stood motionless in the middle of the street, dressed from head to toe in all black mourning attire.

The shrouded figure flagged down the trolley as it approached. The motorman slowed the engine to a dead stop. The conductor nervously asked if she wanted to board.

"No," came a voice behind a dark veil. "I am looking for a man."

"Well, I'm a man," the conductor replied.

"Yes, but you are not the man I am looking for."[49]

With that, the shrouded figure stepped back and disappeared into the shadows. The motorman released the brake, and the trolley lumbered north. The *Muncie Star* reported that "both the conductor and the motorman shivered" at the exchange. The traction workers had just encountered the Woman in Black, a strange figure haunting Southside Muncie in 1907.

Strange sightings started earlier in March around Industry, Muncie's fast-growing suburb to the south. The *Star* wrote in June that "a veritable reign of terror seems to be raging in this usually quiet part of the city, bloodshed has been threatened and the inhabitants do not venture out of their safe retreats."[50] The shadowy figure was "attired from head to foot in colors of jet black, black skirt, black waist, black hat and black veil."[51]

Left: A ghostly figure from the 1865 book *Spectropia*. *Courtesy of the Wellcome Collection.*

Below: Avondale streetcar in front of Beech Grove Cemetery's front gate, early 1900s. *Courtesy of Jeff Koenker.*

Opposite: Muncie in the 1904. *Courtesy of the Indiana State Library.*

The spirit accosted residents "in the late hours of the night, coming out from dark nooks, and peering carefully into their faces, and then, apparently satisfied, fade away into the darkness."[52] Muncie police even responded to a report "that the strange woman had been peeping into the windows of a number of residences in Industry."[53]

These near nightly manifestations "frightened a considerable number of residents." Some locals "began to become possessed of the most fearful misgivings," and the "very mention of the 'woman in black' caused tremors of fear to scurry up and down the spinal columns of many."[54] Known victims included Frank Lafferty of the city's board of works, assistant postmaster John Fitzgibbons and Ball Brothers Glass Manufacturing workers Harry Hope and Chris Beck.

At the time, the big neighborhoods south of the Big Four tracks (now CSX) were suburban housing districts built around factories. We may think of Industry, Avondale, Shedtown and Congerville today as urban quarters in Southside Muncie, but at the tail end of the Indiana Gas and Oil Boom in 1907, these neighborhoods formed Muncie's first suburbia.

Muncie ballooned in size after the discovery of natural gas in 1886. The population had quadrupled from a meager 5,219 residents in 1880 to 20,942 in 1900. Investors worked through private organizations like Citizens' Enterprise Company to entice manufacturers and developers to the Magic City. They offered industrialists land to build factories, free natural gas and cash. As a result, dozens of new factories opened during the boom. They in turn hired thousands of people to forge steel, manufacture barbed wire, plate silver, make paper and blow glass.

These new Munsonians needed someplace to live. Developers, working in tandem with

SUBURB IN TERROR; STRANGER AT LARGE

Woman In Black Makes Nightly Appearance, Despite the Threats.

FRIGHTENED A CAB DRIVER

Negro, In Glass Factory, Badly Beaten While Playing Practical Joke.

Headline from the *Muncie Morning Star*, June 9, 1907. *Scanned from microfilm at Ball State University's Bracken Library*.

business owners, responded and platted suburban neighborhoods around or near factory sites along Muncie's rail corridors. The greater part of the Industry neighborhood was platted first in 1887 as the Galliher Subdivision of Muncie. Avondale to the west was platted a year later as the Perkins Addition, while Congerville and Shedtown to the south were developed in stages, circa 1889 to 1900.

Dozens of industries were producing goods in Muncie when the Woman in Black first appeared in 1907. The city's 1907 Emerson Directory listed an automobile gear manufacturer; seventeen bakers; nineteen blacksmiths; a book binder; four bottling works; a canning factory; six carriage manufacturers; dozens of builders and developers; a creamery; brass, steel and iron foundries; eight places to buy guns and ammo; three sawmills; five oil brokers; seven gas and oil well suppliers; and one paper company.[55]

The boom wasn't just in manufacturing—all of Muncie flourished at the turn of the century. By 1907, the city's economy was supporting 5 banks, 1 advertising agency, 3 architects, about 60 practicing attorneys, 50 barbers, 11 bicycle dealers, 6 boardinghouses and 13 hotels, 1 brewery, 3 business colleges, 13 retail clothing shops, 22 general (dry goods) stores, 48 restaurants, 18 livery stables, 21 feed stores, a staggering 141 grocers, 70 butchers and dozens of real estate and insurance agents but only one small

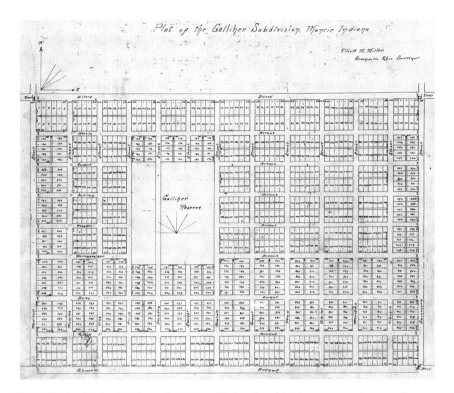

The 1887 plat for the Galliher subdivision of Muncie, which later grew to become the greater part of Industry Neighborhood. *Courtesy of Delaware County, Indiana's Office of Information and GIS Services.*

hospital. Fortunately, Munsonians could seek medical care from any one of sixty-one physicians, most of whom made house calls.

For those looking for a boozy good time, no fewer than one hundred saloons operated in Greater Muncie circa 1907. Come the holy day, residents could atone for libertine nights at any of thirty-seven churches or at Muncie's lone Jewish Temple at the southwest corner of Howard and High Streets.

Residents in 1907 read local news and information from five papers: the *Muncie Evening Press*, the *Muncie Morning Star*, the *Muncie Weekly Herald*, the *Muncie Weekly Times* and the *Observer*. They were entertained at Star Theatre and Wysor Grand, the two leading vaudeville and movie houses of the day, or went to one of Muncie's six movie theaters: Colonial, Nickelodeon, Palace, Royal, Theatorium and Vaudelle. Greater Muncie in '07 was served by Western Union Telegraph, two phone companies, nine photographers, electric streetcar and Interurban mass transit systems and a half dozen intercity steam railroads.

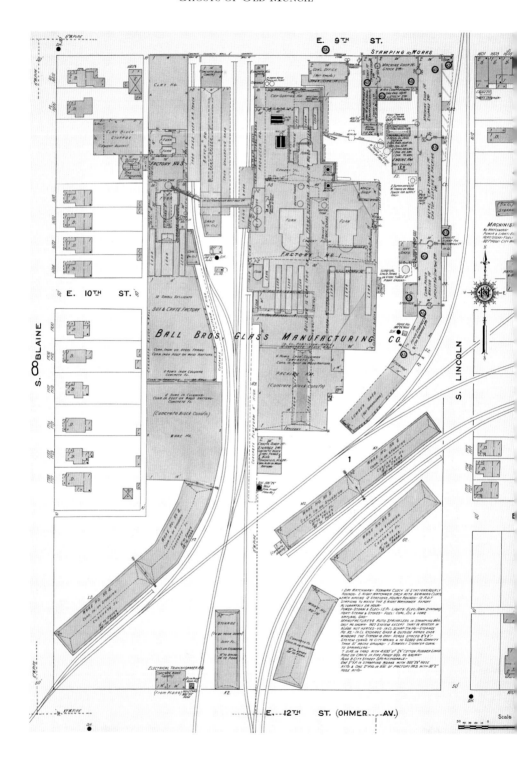

However, of all the industries to come to Muncie during the boom, glass manufacturers had the greatest impact in the era and after. Hemingray, Maring Hart, Muncie Glass, Nelson Glass, Charles Over Glassworks and Port Glass Works all opened shop during the boom, although they didn't survive it. The lone and most notable exception was Ball Brothers Glass Manufacturing. The firm and its founders forever changed Muncie. The company began producing glass here in 1888 and became a dominant economic force in the city throughout the twentieth century.

Citizens' Enterprise had brokered a deal to lure Ball Brothers from Buffalo, New York, in 1887 with $7,500 in cash, rail spurs, free natural gas for five years and land to establish a factory in the southeast corner of Industry.[56] By 1907, the sprawling Ball Brothers Glass factory was making millions of canning jars and employing Munsonians around the clock to produce them.

It was in this thriving world of glass and economic growth that the Woman in Black first appeared. In early June, the *Star* reported that second-shift factory workers at Ball Brothers "have been going home in bunches and scarcely anyone will go anyplace unaccompanied."[57] One evening, the ghostly visitor met face to face—or, more accurately, face to veil—with two men coming home from their night shift. Horrified, the laborers were "thrown in paroxysms of fear by beholding the Woman in Black."[58]

That same night, a cab driver spied the shadowy figure lurking about "the southern part of the city." The terrified cabbie whipped "up his horses and 'beat it' into town" without looking back.[59] The *Star* concluded that "the citizens of Industry are staying indoors more of this time than ever before" and that the Woman in Black "is almost the sole topic of conversation in the suburb…workmen at lunch time discuss her, families discuss her and her name is repeated time and again on the street."[60]

No one really knew what she wanted. Most interactions happened in total silence. Ball Brothers worker D.C. Darst said as much mid-June. On his walk home from a second shift, Darst was startled

Sanborn Fire Insurance map showing the Ball Brothers Glass Manufacturing plant in 1911. *Courtesy Library of Congress.*

"when he saw the black form approaching in the middle of the street. The two brushed clothing but not a word was exchanged."[61]

Darst told a reporter, "Really, I never believed the story that was going the rounds, but I certainly believe it now. She was dressed from head to foot in black and wore a black veil. She seemed deeply concerned about something. I feared saying anything to her."[62]

That same week, four other Ball Brothers' workers out on lunch one evening "met the strange lady in a dark place." They "sprinted to the nearest home and remained there the rest of the night." Once safely inside, they phoned the foreman to explain their tardiness. He told them to return or be fired. The frightened glass men chose to forfeit their jobs.[63]

Although some Southsiders feared a ghostly apparition, others suspected mischief of a human origin. Rumors circulated almost from the start that the Woman in Black was a "man parading in the streets, enjoying the sensation he is creating. Others say the strange female is a woman who is looking for someone who has wronged her."[64] Witness statements were inconclusive.

In mid-June 1907, two glassmakers met the phantom in Heekin Park on their way home from work. When they later told the story, they couldn't recall any identifying feature because the "large black veil that hid her face prevented ascertaining whether the person was a man or a woman."

Some Southsiders weren't taking chances. The *Star* wrote that many "[i]ndustry residents, it is said, go armed at night and some have expressed themselves that if they come in contact with the woman, they will encounter a force and put an end to the hideous nights in the suburb."[65] Armed search parties had "been organized to hunt for the creature, but thus far she has been able to elude all intended captors."[66]

WOMAN IN BLACK TERRORIZES SUBURB

Hair-Raising Experiences Have Thoroughly Alarmed the Residents.

FACTORY MEN FRIGHTENED

All Efforts to Identify Mysterious Creature Have Been Futile.

Headline from the *Muncie Morning Star*, June 7, 1907. *Scanned from microfilm at Ball State University's Bracken Library.*

PRACTICAL JOKERS IN SERIOUS PRANK

Dummy Representing "Woman In Black," Frightened the Pedestrians.

AGED WOMAN PROSTRATE

Industry Is In a Frenzy as Result of the Nightly Visitations.

Headline from the *Muncie Morning Star*, June 14, 1907. *Scanned from microfilm at Ball State University's Bracken Library.*

Heekin Park in the early twentieth century. *Courtesy of Ball State University Libraries' Bracken Archive and Special Collections.*

The hauntings also attracted Muncie's pranksters. On June 9, a worker at Ball Brothers "decided that he would take advantage of the fear permeating the vicinity and play a joke on a friend."[67] The troublemaker, dressed in all black, tiptoed behind his colleague and "tapped him lightly on the shoulder."[68] The terrified friend turned and, without hesitation, hit the imposter upside the head with a shovel.

A week later, a group of boys "rigged up a dummy and placed it against a fence on South Penn street. It was dressed in black clothes and had about the top a heavy black veil, the same as is worn by the Woman in Black."[69] An old woman passing by was "seized with fright and fell to the sidewalk."[70] A few others "took to their heels" and ran home.

The more curious Munsonians stayed to gawk at the uncanny prank. When Muncie Police patrolman Clayton Blakely came upon the scene, the dummy hung motionless, save for the black veil moving gently in the breeze. "No one else in the crowd had the nerve to approach the object."[71] Blakely laughed and pulled the effigy's black dress, causing straw to tumble out. The mob laughed at the antics and went home. The *Star* cautioned readers, "Even though the dummy was routed, the Woman in Black remains at large."[72]

A rumor floated at the end of the month that three men from Industry had tackled the Woman in Black in Heekin Park one evening. Like an end to a *Scooby-Doo* episode, they pulled back the veil to reveal "a prominent businessman, having an uptown office."[73] Southside scuttlebutt at the time had it that this man was attempting to shadow his wife, who may have been cheating on him. After the unveiling in Heekin Park, the faux Woman in Black swore the captors to secrecy. Perhaps after a bribe to keep quiet, the ghost was let go.

It's hard to know what, exactly, to make of all this more than a century later. Someone or something dressed in women's black mourning attire was certainly terrorizing Muncie Southsiders, but who? The *Muncie Star* reported, "Dr. [David] Goodnight, an optician who has offices uptown, believes that he is under suspicion."[74]

Someone sent him a letter accusing him of being the Woman in Black, but the good Dr. Goodnight adamantly denied it. He told a *Star* reporter that he was "not connected with the case in any way and desires that his statement shall put an end to any rumor that might connect his name with the affair."[75]

In late July, a vaudeville juggler named Thomas Austin claimed that he and a companion came across the Woman in Black. In town for a show at Muncie's Star Theatre (Muncie Civic today), Austin was escorting a friend home through Industry when they "unexpectedly came upon the strange individual."

The Woman in Black was now armed. She "drew a revolver from the folds of her dress and ordered him to walk to the nearby corner."[76] Austin's female companion fled, but the juggler complied. The Woman in Black scrutinized "his features for a moment" and then "let him go on his way."[77]

By August, the whole affair had become a joke. The Muncie Electric Light Company even took out an ad in the *Muncie Star*, boldly proclaiming that it had vanquished the Woman in Black. One evening, she popped by the company headquarters when, all of a sudden, the company's lights "burst forth from the office of the Muncie Electric Light and Sales Room." MEL's showroom radiance caused the Woman in Black to "disappear and vanish."[78]

WOMAN IN BLACK AGAIN IN EVIDENCE

Mysterious Nocturnal Creature Has Renewed Her Terrifying Rambles and Visits.

SEEN AT GARBAGE PLANT

Assistant Superintendent Has a Harrowing Experience.

Headline from the *Muncie Morning Star*, September 23, 1907. *Scanned from microfilm at Ball State University's Bracken Library.*

The New Star Theatre, Muncie, Ind.

The Star Theatre in 1908. *Courtesy of Ball State University Libraries' Bracken Archive and Special Collections.*

The hauntings stopped in early September. The *Muncie Evening Press* wrote an editorial mid-month, asking "what has become of the woman in black?" Despite increased police patrols and vigilant residents, the Woman in Black seemed to have disappeared. The *Press* concluded that "the real identity of the person probably will never be known."[79]

Alas, the *Press* spoke too soon. She reappeared a week later, veiled and searching from the shadows. The *Star* reported on September 23 that "the hideous creature of the nights in Industry—the mysterious Woman in Black—has extended her nocturnal perambulations once more."[80] In this second round of hauntings, she paid a visit to Edward Hafkemeyer, the assistant superintendent of the city's garbage dump on South Hackley Street. Hafkemeyer "relates a most unusual as well as exciting experience with Industry's woman devil."[81]

Hafkemeyer said that he was working late one evening when the Woman in Black approached him outside. She hissed from behind her dark veil, "Come here, I want to see you." The garbage man complied, stepping into the light. The Woman in Black eyed him suspiciously and muttered, "No, you are not the man I want" and then left.[82]

After stopping the Congerville trolley a week later, the Woman in Black was spotted by Charles Johnson at Hoyt and Eighth Streets on October 11. One day later, Alta Hayworth and Grace Phillips were traveling back from Muncie on the Heekin Park trolley when they saw a "somber-clad form of the woman, who was sitting beneath a tree. No words passed between the young women and the strange creature in mourning."[83] By mid-October, Munsonians were routinely spotting the Woman in Black nightly in Shedtown and Avondale.

The hauntings spread across east-central Indiana that fall. In late August, the good people of Dunkirk "were shadowed by the ghostly creature, who made it her business to peek in at the windows and walk across the porches, frightening many persons."[84] In Hartford City, a saloon keeper named Al Mills "saw a tall woman dressed in black standing at the corner of Kickapoo and Cherry streets."[85] Caspar Campbell encountered the

"WOMAN IN BLACK" GRABS ANOTHER MAN

Somber Specter Appears Near Daleville and Works Her Customary Trick.

COUNTRYSIDE IS ALARMED

Gaunt Person Believed to Be Hartford City's "Bogey."

Headline from the *Muncie Morning Star*, October 1, 1907. *Scanned from microfilm at Ball State University's Bracken Library.*

MEN HELD IN SPELL BY WOMAN IN BLACK

Traders in Country Store at Bethel Were Given Severe Fright.

NO ONE DARED TOUCH HER

Stared Into Faces and Disappeared in Darkness.

Headline from the *Muncie Morning Star*, October 7, 1907. *Scanned from microfilm at Ball State University's Bracken Library.*

Woman in Black near Daleville. During the encounter, the creature grabbed Campbell's arm to pull him into a streetlight. She let him go after examining his face and "vanished in the dark."[86]

Sherman Downey and Will Hampson encountered the Woman in Black riding a Union Traction Interurban along Kilgore Avenue. As the car made it into town near Beech Grove Cemetery, the lights revealed a dark figure "going at a nervous and excited pace in the direction of Muncie."[87]

In early October, six residents of Harrison Township gathered at Frank Dotson's store in Bethel to chit-chat the evening away. At about 9:00 p.m., the Woman in Black silently walked into the establishment. Dotson told the *Star*:

She looked at the faces of all of us and got to within four or five feet of the stove, when she turned around and walked out. She was dressed from head to foot in black and wore a black veil that did not extend below her nose. I took a good view of her countenance and observed her form. Her cheek bones were prominent, her cheeks sunken and pale. She was more than five feet in height and weighed about 120 or 125 pounds.[88]

Theories and rumors swirled through the end of the year, but the hauntings were never explained. The *Evening Press* tried by publishing a fantastic theory from an unnamed New York City visitor. The mysterious "expert" suggested that the Woman in Black was a member of the ruthless Black Hand Society. "He predicted that in all probability, there would be a mysterious murder and then there would be no more heard from the character."[89]

Captain Hamilton Beall of the Muncie Police had a different theory and claimed to know the identity of the Woman in Black. He told the *Star*, "At the present time, I do not care to tell the name of the person, but I will say that it is a man who dresses as a woman, and who runs about the suburb for no other purpose than to frighten people for the fun of it."[90] Beall even advised Munsonains to "carry a club or something and use it unsparingly on the night wanderer."[91]

The last report of the Woman in Black happened on October 13, when a musician named Cameron Drummond became "the latest victim of the woman in black." He was walking east on Jackson Street when "a black form stalked across his way." Drummond felt her presence before he saw her, but it "was then too late to escape."[92] She disappeared into the shadows, never to be seen again.

David Goodnight, the optician accused of being the Woman in Black in the spring of 1907, was sued for divorce by his wife, Flora, at the end of the year. Flora claimed that Goodnight had an "uncontrollable temper and has frequently cursed and beat her." Flora's attorneys argued that Goodnight had failed to take her to church and, most relevant to our story, "was out nearly every night until late hours and sometimes did not come home during the entire night."[93] Judge Joseph Leffler granted the divorce on Christmas Eve when Dr. Goodnight failed to appear in court.

He had vanished, one might say, just like the Woman in Black.

KNOWS WHO "SHE" IS

CAPTAIN BEALL'S CLAIM

Muncie Policeman Says He's **Ascertained** Identity of the **"Woman in Black."**

Police Captain Hamilton Beall has

Headline from the *Muncie Morning Star*, October 1, 1907. *Scanned from microfilm at Ball State University's Bracken Library.*

CHAPTER 3

AN ICEHOUSE GHOST RETURNS

In mid-August 1892, a ghost began haunting the grounds of the Muncie Ice Company plant on North Elm Street. The *Muncie Morning News* reported that "for the past three weeks some of the employees of the ice factory and our northside citizens have been talking about a ghostlike figure that wanders around Wysor's Field."[94] The ghost appeared every night, "so say the informants, about 11 o'clock and remains about three hours."[95] The nightly specter would float around an old maple tree, just north of the icehouse, and then disappear. One eyewitness even claimed to have seen the spirit about twenty times that summer.

Another unnamed icehouse worker said that the ghost's haunting was anticipated. "I have been expecting him since summer....This is the fourth or fifth time that I can remember of, and it is always every seventh summer."[96]

Four *Muncie Morning News* reporters became so enamored of the story that, one evening, they attempted "to interview the Ice House Spook."[97] They gathered with a few icehouse workers "on the shady side of the ice factory… and then all commenced to survey the situation."[98] Just past 11:00 p.m., "There it was. Not over one hundred yards away, shining forth in a misty dull lightness beneath the tree was a tall, ghostlike figure. It appeared as stationary as a statue."[99]

After some deliberation, the ghost hunters decided to approach the shade, but it "faded away" as soon as they moved toward it. As the group walked back, "They turned and there was the grim figure, right in the same place."[100]

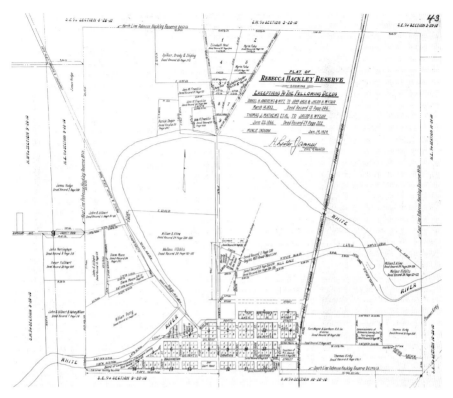

Lester Janney's 1929 plat map showing the Hackley Reserve and land sales of Goldsmith Gilbert and his heirs. *Courtesy of Delaware County, Indiana's Office of Information and GIS Services.*

Icehouse workers had a field day with the sightings and spun all kinds of yarn. One worker told a reporter:

> *You see, right where the ice plant stands there used to be a graveyard. The ghost story, as I remember it being told by my grandmother, is that of Goldsberry Gilbert, one of the first settlers in this county, who died well over forty years ago. This man Gilbert was buried here by the ice plant. He was a great power among the Indians in his day, having built his home right in the midst of their settlement down where Wysor's mill now stands.*
>
> *After [Gilbert's] death, the Indians claim that his ghost wandered over the river bottoms every night, and since then the story of its re-appearance every seven years has been told and re-told.*[101]

Arthur Rackham's "One Grasshopper Spring." *Courtesy of Old Book Illustrations.*

Most of the area around Muncie Ice Company's plant was known at the time as "Wysor's Bottoms"—an informal name given to the area within the river bend north of Wysor Street. Over the years, locals gave the flood-prone region other nicknames, like the "Low North End," "Wysor's Fields" or "Wysor's Bottom Lands." Flooding stopped after the U.S. Army Corps of Engineers completed the levee system around 1950. But in 1892, when the ghost appeared, Wysor's Bottoms was mostly cow pasture and undeveloped floodplains.

Prior to American colonization, the Bottoms and all of what we now call Delaware County was home to Lenape (Delaware) Native Americans. The Lenape established about a dozen villages along the West Fork of the White River between 1796 and 1821, three of which existed in what is now Delaware County: Wapikamicoke, Old Town Hill or Buckongahelas' Town near Inlow Springs; Wapikamikunk or Munsey Town on the north bluff overlooking the river bend at what is now Minnetrista Museum and Gardens; and Owenachki or Hockingpomsga's Town at Priest Ford Road in Mount Pleasant Township.

The Lenape were forced away from their ancestral homeland along the East Coast by Euro-American colonists. By the American Revolutionary War, many lived scattered across Pennsylvania and northern Ohio. Several bands allied after the war with Odawa, Shawnee, Wyandot and Myaamia (Miami) Native Americans to fight against U.S. colonization west of the Allegheny Mountains. Despite several early military successes, the tribes were defeated and relinquished most of Ohio to the federal government. As a result, the Lenape had no place to go. Their Myaamia allies invited several bands of Munsee and Unami-speaking Lenape to live on the West Fork of the White River.

After the War of 1812, the federal government coerced both Myaamia and Lenape to "relinquish title" on huge tracts of land in central Indiana in the 1818 treaties at St. Marys, Ohio. The White River Lenape relocated to Missouri around 1820. Known as the New Purchase, the Native land in Indiana obtained from the treaties was carved up, divided into counties and sold mostly to white settlers at low prices on easy credit.

The Myaamia treaty at St. Marys included land reservations for prominent chiefs and their descendants, one of whom was Rebekah Hackley, the granddaughter of Myaamia chief Mihšihkinaahkwa (Little Turtle). The treaty granted Hackley "one section of land, to be located at the Munsey town, on White river, so that it shall extend on both sides to include three hundred and twenty acres of the prairie, in the bend of the river, where the bend assumes the shape of a horse shoe."[102]

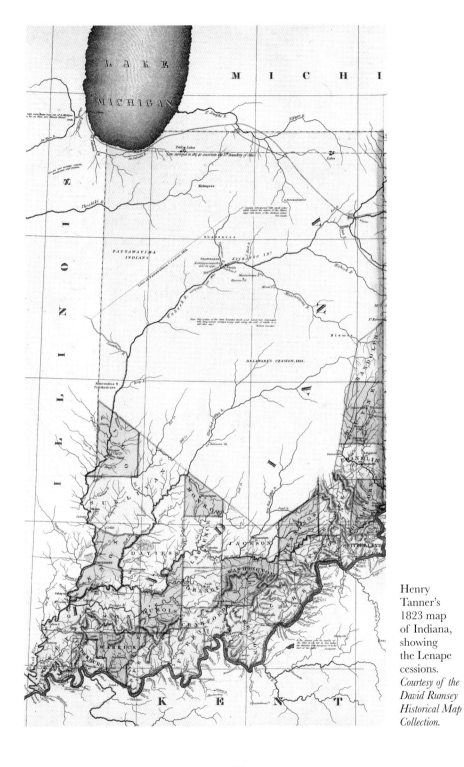

Henry Tanner's 1823 map of Indiana, showing the Lenape cessions. *Courtesy of the David Rumsey Historical Map Collection.*

Hackley sold her reserve in 1825 to Goldsmith and Mary Gilbert, married settlers who ran a trading post along the Mississinewa River at the time. Goldsmith, hailing from upstate New York, with Mary from Ohio, first settled along Prairie Creek around 1820. Although their trading house was located along a well-worn old trail between Muncie and Connersville, the swampy wetlands surrounding Prairie Creek limited travelers. The Gilberts moved to establish a second post along the Mississinewa River, a bit southeast of present-day Eaton in Delaware County.

Hon. GOLDSMITH C. GILBERT
DIED JAN. 20TH 1844

Goldsmith Gilbert. Engraving is from Thomas Helm's *History of Delaware County* (1881). *Courtesy of the Delaware County Historical Society.*

According to county historian Thomas Helm, the Gilberts were attacked at the Mississinewa post by an unnamed group of Native Americans, "who set fire to his house and store, burned up all he owned."[103] I'm confident there is more to this story than what the historical record provides, but the Indian agent at Fort Wayne deducted a penalty from the unnamed tribe's annuity to compensate the Gilberts. Goldsmith used this money to buy Rebekah Hackley's reserve in 1825.[104] Two years later, he donated some of this land to the State of Indiana with two other settlers to form Muncietown as Delaware County's seat of justice.

It's fitting that "Goldsberry" Gilbert would haunt the icehouse in 1892, for the whole stretch of Muncie along Wysor Street, from what is now the Dr. Martin Luther King Jr. Boulevard Bridge on the east to the Muncie Field House west, was once Goldsmith Gilbert's domain.

Gilbert dug an east–west millrace here around 1830, just north and approximately parallel to what is now Wysor Street. Along the race and near the intersection of Wysor and Walnut Streets, Gilbert established grain and saw mills, a woolen factory, a blacksmith and a distillery. Gilbert also opened an inn and had a stake in a dry goods store. His house sat where American Legion Post No. 19 is today.

GILBERT SERVED ONE TERM in the Indiana General Assembly as a representative but died in 1844 on his way home from that year's session.[105] His land,

Jacob Henry Wysor. Engraving is from Thomas Helm's *History of Delaware County* (1881). *Courtesy of the Delaware County Historical Society.*

including all the Hackley Reserve, was sold to Jacob Wysor, an early Muncie industrialist and real estate investor. By the Civil War, the dry high ground northeast of the river bend had become known as Wysor's Heights and the flood-prone land south within the bend, Wysor's Bottoms.

After the railroads arrived in Muncie, a spur called the Jerusalem Track was added to service the mills in Wysor's Bottoms. New factories opened along the spur, including Wysor and Kline's Mill near what is now Star Bank. The spur also serviced Muncie Ice Company, located in the building that is now Elm Street Brewing Company.

Muncie Ice was formed sometime around 1880 and operated a facility north of Washington Street on Muncie's east end. The ice vendors originally sold blocks of lake ice to Munsonians, freshly shipped via train from Warsaw, Indiana. An 1882 ad in the *Muncie Morning News* proclaimed, "The Muncie Ice Company has just received a lot of Pure Lake Ice from the north, which will be furnished to customers in any quantity desired."[106]

The company built a new icehouse in 1891, about a year before the ghost appeared. In March, Muncie Ice directors "yesterday purchased of Jacob Wysor, a lot 150x205 feet just north of the [Jerusalem Track], on which to erect their plant. The plans of the building are all completed.…They expect to have the plant ready for operation by May 1st."[107]

At the time of the haunting in 1892, Muncie Ice used an ammonia process to freeze water. The *Morning Star* described it in 1902:

> *Water will be used to condense the steam from which the ice is eventually frozen and to cool the coils through which the ammonia vapor passes on its way to the ammonia coils in the brine tank, where the cans of ice are frozen.*[108]

The workers and engineers making this "artificial ice" were the ones who saw the seven-year icehouse ghost in August 1892. Their backstory about Gilbert being a "great power among the Indians in his day," however,

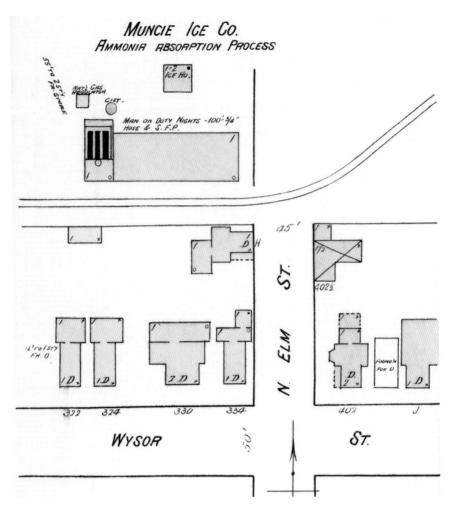

Muncie Ice in 1892, as shown in this Sanborn Fire Insurance Map. *Courtesy Library of Congress.*

is historically nonsensical. The Lenape had all left by the time Gilbert established his Muncietown in 1827. And no one, especially not the area's Native population in the early 1820s, believed Gilbert to be a great power.

Nevertheless, the part of the story about Goldsmith Gilbert being buried in a cemetery "right where the ice plant stands" is, in fact, true. A small graveyard existed at the corner of Wysor and Elm Streets in the 1830s and early 1840s. It's unclear how many people were buried here in Muncietown's first non-Native cemetery, but locals had interred several Gilbert family members, along with the man himself.[109] Supposedly, all the bodies were disinterred and reburied at Beech Grove Cemetery sometime in the 1840s.

Wysor's Bottoms, looking south from what is now Minnetrista Museum and Gardens. *Courtesy of the Delaware County Historical Society, Mike Mavis Collection.*

Almost all of them, that is. A century later in 1948, a Munsonian by the name of Walter Hughes was digging out his basement for a new furnace at 317 East Wysor Street. About two hours into the job, Hughes uncovered two one-hundred-year-old human skeletons in a wooden coffin underneath his basement floor. His house was about a half block south of the old Muncie Ice Company plant on North Elm.[110]

If twentieth-century pop culture has taught us anything of value, it's that we should never, *ever* build anything over an old cemetery. Absolutely nothing good will come from it. If it wasn't Gilbert haunting the good people of Muncie every seven years, it might have been someone else left behind in his old cemetery.

When the icehouse ghost appeared in summer of 1892, "Every mother's son…was immediately seized with 'buck ague.' Their knees knocked together and their teeth rattled like hail on an iron roof."[111] When it first appeared, the specter approached a group of workers, "nearer and nearer it came and the watchers, to their utter astonishment, saw it disappear."[112]

On August 13, 1892, the *Muncie Evening Press* wrote that a Muncie Ice engineer named Albert Squires spotted the ghost. However, Squires believed that it wasn't the spirit of Gilbert but rather an old coworker named Joe Edmonds:

> *Night before last Squires was gazing out into the night and saw what appeared to him a white, moving object. He watched the object closely and it is said that it was the form of Joseph Edmonds, a former engineer employed at the plant, who died about eight months ago.*[113]

Left: Mary J. Edmonds, daughter of Goldsmith and Mary Gilbert and the wife of Uncle Joe Edmonds. Engraving is from Thomas Helm's *History of Delaware County* (1881). *Courtesy of the Delaware County Historical Society.*

Right: Édouard de Beaumont's 1871 etching, "Ghosts of His Own Making." *Courtesy of Old Book Illustrations.*

Edmonds, a Muncie Ice engineer and night watchman, had died earlier in January from heart failure. His body was found in bed at Vickery's Boarding House and Saloon, 322 Wysor Street. When "Mrs. Vickery went to awake him, she found that he was cold in death."[114]

Known affectionately to Munsonians of the era as "Uncle Joe," Edmonds was described by the *Muncie Daily Herald* as "true friend to his friends" and "solid as a rock." He was a "staunch Democrat" and had spent forty of his sixty-two years in Delaware County.[115] Edmonds worked at Wysor and Kline for decades before his employment at Muncie Ice. He was also well connected, having married Goldsmith and Mary Gilbert's daughter Mary Jane.

Alas, whoever was haunting Muncie that year never returned, not in 1899, 1906, 1913, 1920 or any seventh year thereafter. An icehouse haunting was never reported in the press during those years. I looked back at news reports in 1885 but found nothing. Perhaps this is because the reporters covering the story in 1892 concluded that the icehouse wasn't actually being haunted by Gilbert or Edmonds after all.

The newsmen determined that the uncanny "misty white object" that caused so much excitement that summer was nothing more than "an old rag hanging on the fence."[116]

CHAPTER 4

AVONDALE'S HAUNTED HOUSE AT NINTH AND HOYT

In the summer of 1905, a ghost began haunting the residents of Muncie's Avondale neighborhood. The apparition manifested in a dilapidated house on the southwest corner of Hoyt and Ninth Streets. The *Muncie Morning Star* reported that "at midnight, a ghostly figure appears within. So the story goes, the spook is that of a woman, an Italian, who died in the house years ago. She is wont to appear at a front window, shriek and dissolve into the darkness."[117]

For months, groups of boys passing the house at night claimed "to have heard a woman shriek and fall."[118] One night in late winter, a group of kids were walking down Ninth Street when "suddenly, as they neared the front of the structure, a weird moan was heard and the gaunt white form of a woman appeared in a front window of the empty house with a wild shriek and the figure waved its hand aloft, then fell."[119]

The group "stopped speechless with horror and then fled."[120] The next day, the boys told everyone they knew in Avondale about what happened, and "the story spread over the entire neighborhood. Some hooted the idea of a ghost and hinted the gang had taken 'too much' at the beverage emporium they left at almost midnight."[121] "But by far, the majority believed that hoodoo clung to the house."[122]

Most residents just avoided the place, given its condition. The papers suggested that its tumbledown state may have fostered such ghostly sightings, "the broken windows, unhinged doors, and decaying veranda are decidedly suggestive of the uncanny."[123] Trash laid scattered about

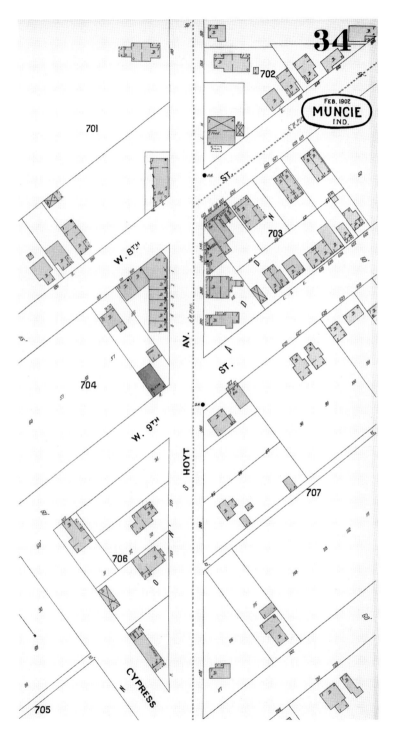

34

FEB. 1902
MUNCIE
IND.

Hoyt and Ninth
Street in 1902.
*Courtesy Library
of Congress.*

the property, and thieves had scavenged the locks and metal fixtures. The "deserted and dilapidated cottage in Muncie bears testimony to the force of superstition."[124] Every society has such tales, the *Star* told readers, but "reason and facts are put to flight in these ghost stories, which find their chief attractiveness in weirdness."[125]

The house in question sat near the intersection of Hoyt Avenue and Ninth Street in Southside Muncie's Avondale neighborhood. At the time of the haunting in 1905, the intersection was home to a half dozen houses, a barn, James Shinn's Blacksmith and Cannady's Grocery, which doubled at night as a saloon.

Hoyt Avenue, just as it is today, was a major thoroughfare leading travelers into and out of Muncie on the city's southwest side. Hoyt's route through town was built many years before in 1832 as the Pendleton Road. The Indiana General Assembly had commissioned the highway that year to connect Muncietown with Pendleton. The road was part of a statewide effort to improve inter-city transportation. Many years later, a U.S. postal carrier reminisced that the Pendleton Road "was laid with poles and logs and was pretty rough."[126]

After the Civil War, the Muncie and Middletown Turnpike Company paved the street as part of a new gravel highway. It connected Muncie, which had just incorporated as a city in 1865, to Middletown in Henry County. From there, Munsonians could travel south to Pendleton and then on to Indianapolis. The route out of Muncie was known thereafter as Middletown Pike. During the gas boom, the pike's course through city limits was officially renamed "Hoyt Avenue."

In the decade after the Civil War, Middletown Pike sliced at an angle through Muncie Driving Park, a horse racetrack located on the farm of Dr. Robert Winton. Today, the track is a loop between Ninth, Pierce, Eleventh and Gharkey Streets. An 1878 ad lists the track as the "best half-mile track in Indiana." William Petty served as superintendent. You can still see the curvature of the loop today at the rounded corner of Eleventh and Pierce Streets.

After the arrival of the Indianapolis and Bellefontaine Railroad in 1852, some farmers in Center Township south of Muncie began marketing their land as residential and commercial property. In the early 1870s, the Muncie Driving Park and the rest of Winton's farm were platted as a residential neighborhood and named Winton Place. The discovery of natural gas in 1886 prompted an acceleration of this type of growth across the city's southside.

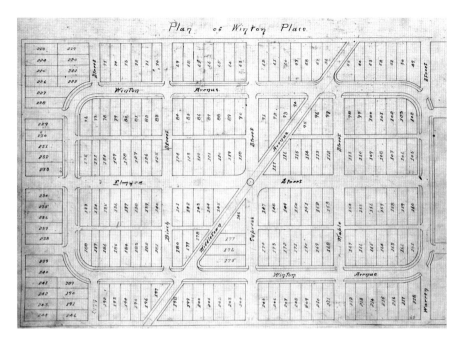

1874 plat map of Winton Place. The Middletown Pike/Hoyt Avenue bisects the old horse track at an angle. *Courtesy of Delaware County, Indiana's Office of Information and GIS Services.*

The John Perkins Addition in 1888 was one of the first such developments. About one year later, Perkins was renamed Avondale for marketing purposes—so chosen as an homage to a Cincinnati suburb of the same name. The Avondale Land Company formed to market and sell lots to developers and new factory workers moving into the city. Muncie's original Avondale neighborhood was bounded by Kilgore Avenue north, Pierce east, Twelfth south and Port Street west.

Avondale grew rapidly. In October 1889, the *Muncie Morning News* reported:

> *There is no suburb contiguous to Muncie that is improving more rapidly than Avondale. One year ago here were but two or three houses in this beautiful suburb, but to-day one hundred are already erected, and fifty are in the course of construction. Streets and alleys are laid out, sidewalks are being put up to accommodate residents. Avondale is a beautiful place and within the next twelve months it will contain no less than one thousand people.*[127]

Around 1900, the land just north of old Avondale between Eighth Street and the tracks was known informally as "Forty Acres." Later in the

Left: Plat of the Perkins Addition to Muncie, 1888. The development was later renamed Avondale. *Courtesy of Delaware County, Indiana's Office of Information and GIS Services.*

Right: Promotional plat for the Avondale Addition to Muncie. *Courtesy of Ball State University Libraries' Bracken Archive and Special Collections.*

twentieth century, it was home to General Motors' sprawling Chevy plant. However, at the time of the haunting in 1905, Forty Acres was largely undeveloped. Any house east of it was prone to wind damage and perhaps also ghosts. The haunted house at Ninth and Hoyt was located immediately southeast of Forty Acres. The *Star* wrote on June 25, 1905, "Children and matrons regard the dilapidated structure with superstitious interest and after nightfall, fear to go near, while the wind from Forty Acres does its share of making the ghost real by playing mournful tunes over the loose weatherboarding and whistling through open windows."[128]

The house so spooked neighbors that they started calling cops on nights when hauntings got out of hand. Muncie Police patrolman Oscar Furr arrived one evening in late June to "an excited and awed crowd of youngsters with a number of women surrounding the dilapidated cottage in which it is said a full-fledged spook holds its nightly vigils."[129] Furr calmly walked in and found nothing out of the ordinary. He came out of the house and told everyone to go home.

One week later, Muncie Police detective Charles White was "dispatched to 'lay' the night visitor. He found on his arrival that the entire neighborhood had turned out to either dispel the superstition or see the ghost."[130] The city's police department was alarmed at the growing crowds, "with lanterns and sticks, almost a score of men and boys were patrolling the vacant structure intent on 'laying the ghost.'"[131]

Muncie's police sent a detective again because "with torches and clubs, the boys and men were making the night hideous with their efforts to conjure the spirit."[132]

When White arrived, he was "informed by the ghost hunters that they intended staying in the dwelling until midnight, the hour the spirit is reported to be in the habit of appearing."[133] One of the ghostbusters told the *Star* that the spirit was that of an immigrant woman who once lived in the house with her family:

> *Foreigners were the last tenants to occupy the dwelling three years ago. Her death occurred from mysterious causes, suicide suspected, because of an unhappy love affair. It is said she appears on the stroke of 12 in a front window of the house and, throwing her hands aloft, falls to the floor with a shriek. Some residents in the neighborhood fear to pass the decaying old structure after dusk.*[134]

I looked for an early twentieth-century report of a suicide at or near that corner but found nothing. It's certainly possible that the house was once home to an Italian American immigrant family. Historically, Muncie never had a large foreign-born population on par with communities like Indianapolis and Cincinnati, but the Indiana Gas and Oil Boom (1886–1910) attracted workers from many countries, albeit in small numbers. Around 1900,

The haunted house at Ninth and Hoyt, *Muncie Morning Star*, July 30, 1905. *Scanned from microfilm at Ball State University's Bracken Library.*

Muncie newspapers referenced small enclaves of Romanians, Irish, eastern Europeans, Italians and Welsh immigrants throughout the city.

On the night of the ghost hunt in 1905, nothing appeared to the angry mob of Munsonians standing under torchlight. Everyone eventually went home, but the hauntings continued. In mid-August, MPD patrolman Hamilton Beall had "the honor of 'laying' the mystic nightly visitor, which for weeks has filled small folk of the neighborhood with superstitious awe."[135] It was Beall's turn to try and ascertain what was going on. The police were tired of being called "to the vicinity at various times because of disturbances by parties of ghost hunters."[136]

Unlike his colleagues, Patrolman Beall located the source of the haunt. He "discovered the ghost was no more than the weird light thrown in an uncanny manner from a neighboring streetlight on the white interior of the dwelling."[137]

A *Star* reporter was on the scene: "The spook came, about the time the moon became hidden behind a bank of dark clouds, the city lights lighted with a sputter and flash." Beall stated that "he observed that a light one block south on Tenth Street could be seen only when the breeze parted the dense foliage of trees between the house." As the wind blew the branches open, "rays of light passed through a rear window…throwing a wavering light on the white-washed walls."[138]

"The belief that the ghost came only on stormy nights was explained, as the wind blows strongly enough to part the branches," the *Star* concluded. Patrolman Beall believed that "he has 'played' the ghost, as do a large number of residents." But not everyone was so sure; some "insist that a more substantial 'spook' may yet be seen."[139]

However, come November, the *Star* wrote that the "haunted stories are all a matter of history now."[140] Just like "most uncanny spirits, the famous ghost of the Southside has apparently silently faded away. No more will the spook, which, according to the lore of the neighborhood, has haunted the house at Hoyt Avenue and Ninth Street, cast its fearful mystic spell over the dwelling and vicinity."[141]

A brickmaker by the name of Cyrus Crane had purchased the property and moved in with his family. The neighbors were soon "surprised to see the so-called 'haunted house' undergoing repairs." Crane painted the house so well that "not a cottage in the neighborhood presented a more respectable appearance, as some of the housewives remarked in wonder."[142] Crane said that "no unusual sounds have marred or disturbed their peaceful slumber." The brickmaker returned life to the house. In doing so, Crane seemed to have vanquished any malevolent spirits.

The neighbors concurred, now believing that the "ghost was, as usual, a myth and thus has the Southside spirit vanished."[143]

CHAPTER 5

BRIGHT SPIRITS AT RICHWOOD

The small hamlet of Richwood lies a few miles southwest of Muncie on the old Middletown Pike (now Indiana State Road 67). You wouldn't think much of the hamlet today driving through it in the twenty-first century. There's no sign for it, but there is a gas station, modern housing and acres of asphalt and concrete. The interchange just north of Richwood links Hoyt Avenue and the Tillotson Extension to the Muncie Bypass.

Most locals don't even recognize Richwood as a settlement, but in the mid-nineteenth century, the hamlet was a vibrant center of rural Delaware County life. In its prime after the Civil War, Richwood served as a rural crossroads for the Middletown, Rangeline and Daleville turnpikes. The hamlet had a post office sporadically from 1843 to 1890, grocery and general stores, a schoolhouse, a blacksmith, a Methodist church and a toll gate. A small stone bridge carried the Middletown Pike over Jones Ditch, a tributary feeding No Name Creek to the north.

In the days before railroads and interstates, communities like Richwood thrived as hubs of rural country life. Travelers stopped often, especially during busy harvest seasons. Almost everyone in the area farmed, either as landowners or as tenants. Workers temporarily moved in seasonally for planting and harvest, transforming the little rural hamlet into a bustling village.

Permanent residents had urban markets and amenities available in nearby Muncie, which was only a short horse ride northeast on the decently maintained gravel Middletown Turnpike. The 1887 *Atlas of Delaware County*

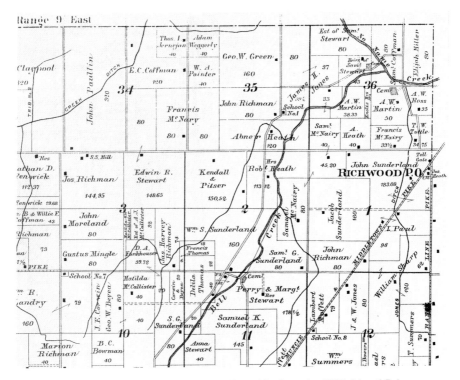

Richwoods in the northeast corner of Salem Township, from the 1887 *Atlas of Delaware County. Courtesy of the Delaware County Historical Society.*

lists several families in the vicinity with surnames like Sunderland, Paul, Sharp, Summers, McNairy, Martin, Tuttle, Ross and Stewart.

The community was never officially platted and has no legal boundaries. In the 1890s, No Name Creek provided an informal border on the hamlet's north and east sides, while Bell Creek served as Richwood's western frontier. Several farmhouses faced the Middletown Pike, which ran at an angle southwest in the direction of Middletown in Henry County. Richwood "ended" south somewhere near Salem Township School No. 8 and Little Bell Creek.

If you can believe it, Richwood wasn't the only settlement in the immediate area. Directly south was Progress, a small railroad hamlet that grew around Sharp's Station. The depot was added in 1903 along the Central Indiana Railway, which connected Muncie to Brazil, Indiana, by way of Anderson, Noblesville and Lebanon. Known commonly as the Midland Route, the track into Muncie brought tons of coal from southern Indiana to feed the city's energy-dependent factories as natural gas ran out.[144]

RES. OF WILLIAM SHARP.
MONROE TP DELAWARE CO. IND.

William Sharp's farm, which later became Sharp's Station. Engraving is from Thomas Helm's *History of Delaware County* (1881). *Courtesy of the Delaware County Historical Society.*

South of Progress was Soccum, another informal hamlet that grew around an 1880 post office named Tabor. Due east of Richwood was the hamlet of Corinth, a tiny settlement with Monroe Township School No. 3 and Corinth United Methodist Church at its core.

It was at this busy crossroads in late winter of 1896 that a ghostly light appeared to the good residents of Richwood, according to an anonymous letter published in the *Muncie Daily Times*. The paper credited the author only as "A Resident." The writer claimed that on the night of Sunday, February 16, two Richwood boys rode out to attend evening church services at Corinth United Methodist nearby. Night had fallen by the time they returned around 9:30 p.m. At the crossroads, "a short distance north of Richwood, they noticed along the highway about fifty yards south of where they were stopped, a short distance north of the old toll house, a bright light."[145]

A light on the highway wasn't unusual, but this one moved…weirdly. The letter described the light as "about the size of a candle floating apparently in the atmosphere." It moved upward in "a peculiar zig-zag motion, changing to and fro and dancing about in the darkness as if it was taking particular delight in freezing the boys' blood."[146] The light "kept up this peculiar witchery a few moments and then stopped still." After a moment, it "exploded upward, throwing out a bright, weird-like glow that lighted up the atmosphere some distance around" and then disappeared.[147] A moment later, it reappeared on the other side of the road.

One of the boys, unnamed in the published letter, hopped out of the buggy and ran home, but the other steeled his courage and coaxed his horse toward the direction of the eerie light. The spook began to move frantically, "bobbing and darting about in sharp angles and short curves until he approached near it, when it stopped and then again, noiselessly exploded with such brilliance it startled his horse."[148]

The kid turned fast and rode home. He initially decided to tell no one, out of fear of being ridiculed. As he put his horse away in the family barn, he saw the light again "near the vicinity of the bridge opposite the old Paul homestead." The uncanny light "repeated its pranks with greater energy, as if there existed some dark mystery about the old bridge that augments its ghostly revels."[149]

For its final evening performance, the ghost divided into two parts, which "shone brightly and would emit at short intervals, pulsations of light sufficient in power to light up the forest trees adjoining the bridge to the west."[150]

Corinth Schoolhouse in the hamlet of Corinth, due east of Richwoods. *Courtesy of Ball State University Libraries' Bracken Archive and Special Collections.*

Swallowing his pride, the kid decided to tell his dad the next day. Any suspicion of doubt was cast away because the unnamed father himself witnessed the spectral apparition the following night. On his way home from Joseph Heath's grocery, "on nearing Mr. Sunderland's, the capricious spark appeared, preceding him along the road, appearing eight different times and keeping up its fiery gymnastics to his great wonder and stopping as before in the vicinity of the bridge." When the father got home, "he called his family to the door and watched the light for some time."

Two other residents from Richwood saw the ghost at about 10:00 p.m. on their way back from Corinth. They met

GHOSTLY

LIGHTS ARE MAKING THE RESIDENTS OF RICHWOODS SHAKE IN THEIR BOOTS.

A Mysterious Spark The Size of a Candle That Dances Over the Highway and Explodes.

The Apparition Supposed to be the Shade of a Farmer, Killed a Year Ago by His Runaway Team at a Bridge—The Apparent Rendezvous of the Spook.

Ghosts from Richwoods making headlines in the *Muncie Daily Times*, February 22, 1896. *Scanned from microfilm at Ball State University's Bracken Library.*

it "north of the old toll house and followed it south to the bridge."[151] About five people in all witnessed the strange apparition in a week.

To assuage fears, "watch meetings are being talked of with headquarters at Joseph Heath's grocery, where an effort will be made to imbibe some courage and lay the spook." Fortified with whiskey, they hoped to "discover among the local ranks some Hamlet who will be willing to seize it be the whiskers and demand its business."[152]

What was this mysterious, haunting light? The letter hinted that it might be the spirit of Joe Bright, who had died strangely on Richwood's Middletown Pike bridge one year before in 1895. "Some of our citizens, who remember that almost one year ago…Joe Bright, a tenant on the farm of Samuel Sunderland, was returning from Muncie when he was thrown from his wagon by his running team and killed at this bridge."[153]

Sam Sunderland had found his tenant dead on the bridge in the small hours of March 30, 1895. The *Muncie Daily Times* reported that "whether Bright committed suicide, was killed by his [horse] team running away or was murdered is not known."[154] After discovering the body, Sunderland sent for Muncie Police and the county coroner.

Since it was the middle of the night, Richwood residents stood guard over the body, no doubt trading theories on how Bright died. When Delaware County coroner Joseph Bowers arrived about five hours later,

Muncie Police superintendent Jim Miller in 1895. *Courtesy of Ball State University Libraries' Bracken Archive and Special Collections.*

"an inquest was held by the light of an old smoky lantern."[155] Bright's face "bore marks of violence, there being four gashes—one over and under each eye. The flesh was cut to the bone, but the skull was not fractured under either of the wounds."[156]

Coroner Bowers speculated that a very drunk Bright lost control of his horses, "which ran away throwing him from the wagon." His head came into violent contact with wheels or hooves as he fell face down in the mud. He lay unconscious and suffocated to death on the old stone bridge.

The police weren't so sure. Patrolman Curtis Turner and Muncie Metropolitan Police superintendent James Miller believed that "Bright had been murdered by someone who used a blunt instrument."[157] Chief Miller told a reporter, "I am almost confident that the man met his death in a foul manner. I am investigating the case and may unearth something startling."[158]

Bright had left Sunderland's farm on the afternoon of March 29 to buy a plow in Muncie, a task he accomplished at W.W. Shirk's on South Walnut Street. On his way back to Richwood, he stopped for a drink at Henry White's saloon in Shedtown. Eyewitnesses saw him in a heated argument with two men, Mike Fierce and John Shockey. The latter threatened to cut Bright up into pieces.[159] The three were supposedly so drunk that White kicked them out.[160]

Bright left and made his way to Enoch Witt's grain mill at Cornbread Road on Buck Creek. He bought the Sunderlands a heavy sack of flour. The mill's attendant said that "Bright was not even staggering" and appeared sober. It was the last time anyone reported seeing him alive.

Later that night in Richwood, Sunderland went looking for Bright at about 2:00 a.m. The tenant's team of two horses had arrived all hot and bothered at the farm without their driver. Sunderland didn't get far before finding Bright dead, his corpse sprawled across the Middletown Pike bridge.[161]

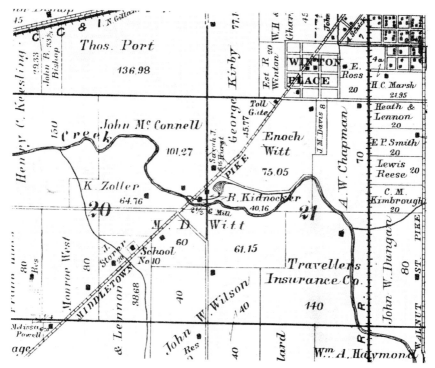

Bright stopped at Enoch Witt's mill southwest of Muncie in Center Township before he headed to Richwoods. From the 1887 *Atlas of Delaware County. Courtesy of the Delaware County Historical Society.*

Local papers covered the investigation for a few weeks, but the story went cold. Given the lack of any evidence suggesting foul play, I'm guessing the case remained unsolved and that Coroner Bower's version of events was generally accepted. Joseph "Joe" Bright was about forty-five years old, married and a father of four. He was buried at Sharp Cemetery along Big Bell Creek southwest of Richwood.

One year later, about a week after the spectral light first appeared, the *Times* published a second anonymous letter from "A Resident," one that perhaps more concretely drove home the subtext of the ghost story. "Some say the light, if followed, would have led to Sharp's cemetery farther south, where the remains of the unfortunate Joe Bright were interred a year ago." The writer added that "the grave of the above deceased when last viewed had the appearance of having been disturbed, which, if true, accounts for the spirit's return and its desire to communicate."[162]

The letter also suggested that "a swift, flying rumor to the effect that the Richwood ghost has been seen again late Saturday night went the rounds in

'I saw two barred eyes looking at me.'

B.E. Minns illustrated this haunting in the 1899 book *Ghosts: Being the Experiences of Flacman Low. Courtesy of the British Library.*

this community Sunday morning."[163] The rumor had spread across southern Delaware County—"the interest in the spook is growing daily, and the details of the strange occurrence are on every tongue."[164]

Skeptics scoffed at such supernatural explanations—"popular belief by those who did not witness the revels of the spook is to the effect that the light belonged to a gas-well heater situated near the road." But unnamed eyewitnesses "stubbornly and emphatically claim that the light was supernatural and could not be the gas well" since it was a half a mile away. Bright's spirit, or whatever it was, "appeared at one time directly west of their position."[165]

The *Times* published this letter on Leap Day, February 29. It's well written, with wonderfully embroidered late Gilded Age American prose. I can't help but quote a paragraph in full:

> *The disquiet spirit will reveal its identity by repeating the scenes of that fateful night in which it will begin at the point on the road above where Bright's horses became unmanageable and came thundering throughout town at a furious speed, mounted in his heavy farm wagon—maybe with and maybe without horses—whooping, hollowing, and moaning, his shaggy black hair, which he wore in life floating wildly in the breeze and all terminating suddenly with a crash and a repetition of the ghastly scene at the haunted bridge. When this is over, the wagon will be changed to a hearse and proceed slowly to the cemetery.*[166]

Another theory was that Bright's "departed spirit" kept returning with "information to divulge and if so, it will continue its visitations, untiringly, until its work is accomplished and its mind set at ease."[167] The writer praised the Richwood ghost hunters, who "expressed on all occasions a reserve of courage and nerve truly admirable."

There are no more reports of Richwood ghost lights thereafter, although someone credited as "A Little Ghost" wrote a letter to the *Daily Times* a few weeks later indicating that the story was a total fake. All anyone had to do, according to Little Ghost, was "hitch up the old family buggy nag and drive down the pike to the gas well some dark night about 12 o'clock," when the "great mystery would be unraveled" to everyone's satisfaction.[168]

One week later, the *Daily Herald* published a very long poem about the spirit of Joseph Bright, penned by an anonymous but "well known young lady." I'll spare you from reading the entire poem, but the first stanza goes:

Near a bridge,
Just o'er the way,
Is a horrible ghost,
So I have heard people say.[169]

Strange occurrences aside, Joe Bright really did die on Richwood's bridge in 1895. Perhaps his ghost returned as a reminder for neighbors to avenge his untimely death. It's also possible that locals were just seeing spirits fading in the final flickers of the gas boom.

CHAPTER 6
THE STONECUTTER'S GHOST OF SELMA PIKE

A few months after Bright's spirit appeared in Richwood, another ghost manifested just east of Muncie on Selma Pike. Today, we call this thoroughfare Indiana State Road 32, but in the summer of 1896, the road was a former turnpike connecting Muncie to the growing village of Selma in Liberty Township. During the gas boom, Selma emerged as a vibrant railroad and oil producing community on Delaware County's east side.

In the early morning of Wednesday, July 22, 1896, an unnamed teamster from Selma set out on the pike toward Muncie to get a load of ice. He headed due west out of Liberty Township, passing numerous farmhouses that faced the graveled highway. The road wasn't used as a turnpike at the time, but locals still called it "Selma Pike" in the 1890s. The route ran parallel to the Big Four Railroad and followed the path of a much older road built by the U.S. federal government in the 1820s. Traffic on the pike in the 1890s was mostly horses, horse and ox carts, buggies and wagons. Selma Pike became Main Street in Muncie, connecting travelers to other highways, railroad stations, shops and markets. Main Street also provided easy access to the Muncie Ice Company's plant via the intersection at Elm Street.

The road into Muncie was well maintained and used by travelers during all hours of the day, including by teamsters before dawn. Morning was the best time to get ice in July—before the sun rose and when traffic was light. For teamsters hauling ice outside of city limits, the plan always was to get into Muncie before dawn, quickly load blocks of ice and then rush home before it all melted in the morning's heat.

A map of Selma from the 1887 *Atlas of Delaware County. Courtesy of the Delaware County Historical Society.*

Such was the pace and mindset of the Selma ice hauler in the summer of 1896. About twenty minutes into his journey, he passed the Delaware County Infirmary, an almshouse and working farm open to those without options. It was known originally as the Delaware County Asylum and colloquially as the "Poor Farm." County commissioners established the infirmary in the 1850s to shelter orphans, residents with debilitating mental illness, elderly without support, impoverished locals and unhoused people. Thomas Helm, the nineteenth-century Delaware County historian, wrote in 1881 that the infirmary provided "the necessaries of life and shielded from the inclemencies of weather, and otherwise treated [residents] according to the dictates of a common humanity."[170]

The institution's imposing edifice was hard to miss coming down the pike into Muncie. As the ice hauler came near, he saw something dark and uncanny lying beneath the giant hickory tree out front by the gate. The

COUNTY INFIRMARY, DELAWARE CO. IND.(LIBERTY TP.)

The original Delaware County Infirmary. Engraving is from Thomas Helm's *History of Delaware County* (1881). *Courtesy of the Delaware County Historical Society.*

Muncie Daily Herald wrote that "yesterday morning, just before daylight, the young Selma resident started to this city after a load of ice. When he neared the big tree, he discovered the body of a man on the ground beneath the spreading branches."[171] It wasn't a man upon closer inspection, according to the hauler, but rather the spirit of one returned.

Many people in Liberty and Center Township were spooked that summer after the mysterious death of Joseph Landers in early July. The *Herald*, which embellished the tale to editorialize, reported that the ice hauler had "thoughts of Landers flash through his brain" and that his "blood fairly froze as he gazed at the body." Terrified, he slapped his horse reins and high-tailed it into Muncie. At the icehouse, he loaded his blocks quickly and headed back to Selma, but "when he returned with the ice it was daylight and nothing unusual was apparent about the tree."[172] A few weeks prior, however, the rising sun revealed a hickory tree in front of the infirmary covered in bloody gore.

In the early morning of Wednesday, July 8, 1896, a farmhand by the name of George Wilson was walking west along the pike toward Muncie. Although he lived near Selma, Wilson worked at the sprawling Claypool Farm on the eastern edge of Center Township. About two miles past the county infirmary, the farmer found a mangled corpse in the middle of Selma Pike.

LANDERS' GHOST ON THE PIKE.

Wierd and Strange Story From the Village of Selma.

A MYSTERIOUS SIGHT

Headline from the Muncie Daily Herald, *July 23, 1896. Scanned from microfilm at Ball State University's Bracken Library.*

"A ghastly find it was," reported the *Herald*. The body was "covered with blood and dirt and presented a horrible appearance."[173] The *Muncie Daily Times* wrote later that day, "Most of the hair on the back of the head was missing, it appeared that the man had been dragged along the road."[174]

The body was lying perpendicular to the pike's east–west main axis. The *Muncie Morning News* wrote that his face "was besmeared with blood and clots of the red fluid matted the hair. The clothes were covered with dust and blood."[175]

Wilson ran to the nearby Meeker Dairy Farm for assistance. A runner was sent to phone police in Boycetown, Muncie's newish working-class east side suburb. Patrolman George Ball, the same cop haunted by William Shumm in the first chapter, was dispatched with Delaware County coroner Joseph Bowers. Ball and Bowers met Sheriff William Sherry at the scene just as the sun breached the horizon.

Bowers closely examined the body. The corpse had a "terrible bruise and cut on his forehead and one on the back of his head. The skin was gone from the left side of his face and his left ear was ground almost off."[176]

Robbery was ruled out. The cops found three dollars in a pocket, along with an unloaded .32-caliber revolver, pipe tobacco and some stationery imprinted with the contact information of Strawder Watson, the infirmary's superintendent. The tattered jacket loosely covering the corpse had the initials "J.L." embroidered on the collar.

Sherry, Ball and Bowers didn't recognize the ruined body but noticed a trail of blood leading up the pike toward the infirmary. Sheriff Sherry and Patrolman Ball headed that way, while Coroner Bowers loaded the mutilated corpse into his wagon and scuttled back to R. Meeks and Sons undertakers at 115 East Main Street in Muncie.

Sherry and Ball followed the blood trail two miles east to the infirmary, where they found a grisly scene. Near the big hickory tree by the front gate, "a big pool of blood was discovered. A trail of blood led to a fence a few feet distant."[177] The gate "was smeared with blood as large as a man's hat and on the inside there was more blood."[178] They also found a jacket with "Jesse Brown" embroidered on the collar. Suspecting foul play, the cops grabbed

Superintendent Watson to help identify the body and made their way back to Muncie.

None of the morticians at Meeks recognized the corpse. With no other way to identify it, the "body was washed and then the curious public was allowed to gaze upon the remains for the purpose of identification."[179] The corpse was "placed on a stretcher for the public to view" out on Main Street, one block east of the courthouse. "Hundreds of people gazed on the dead body."[180]

Given the extensive damage to the face, no one at first recognized who it was, not even Watson, who arrived with Sherry and Ball about 9:00 a.m. But an hour later, "the corpse was identified as that of Joseph Landers, a stone mason aged about fifty."[181]

Around the time Landers's lacerated remains were being put on display at Meeks, "a poor old bay horse attached to a rattle trap of an open wagon, which was covered in blood, was found in an alley near Main and Beacon streets."[182] Locals called police, who sent Patrolman James Cole to investigate. Cole took the rig to McLain's Livery at 225 North Walnut Street. The rickety wagon contained clothing, a bucket of potatoes, wheels of cheese, cooking utensils and a terrified dog with a deep gash under one eye. The *Morning News* described the horse as "blind in one eye and very gentle."[183] The *Herald* reported that "everything including the dog was identified as the property of Landers."[184]

Muncie Police patrolman George Ball in 1895. *Courtesy of Ball State University Libraries' Bracken Archive and Special Collections.*

Just like a block of ice melting in summer sun, Landers's body began to decompose as the balmy July day waned. He was quickly buried in a pauper's grave at Beech Grove Cemetery—"no one but the undertaker and the sexton were present."[185] The *Herald* later reported the results of the postmortem examination: "It is the opinion of the doctors that death was caused by injuries in the region of the brain."[186] He died sometime late Tuesday, July 7, or early the next morning.

Landers had been well known about town as a curmudgeon, a "very irritable and quick tempered man."[187] The papers described him as about

Starlings plagued the third Delaware County Courthouse in the mid-twentieth century. *Courtesy of the Delaware County Historical Society, Mike Mavis Collection.*

fifty years old, "of good size,"[188] with a dark beard and thick mustache. Landers had moved to Muncie in the mid-1880s after being hired by contractors Charles Pierce and Thomas Morgan to help build the ornate, third Delaware County Courthouse. The *Muncie Morning Star* reminisced in 1911:

> *Three years were spent in the construction of this imposing edifice, including the time taken to demolish the modest little brick building which was formerly the Delaware county courthouse. The present structure is one of the most substantial county buildings in the Hoosier state and this is due to the manner in which it was erected.*[189]

Pierce and Morgan also built grand courthouses in Lafayette, Frankfort, Tipton and Franklin. In Muncie, they built the Anthony and Willard blocks, the Johnson block and the Delaware County Infirmary. The firm hired

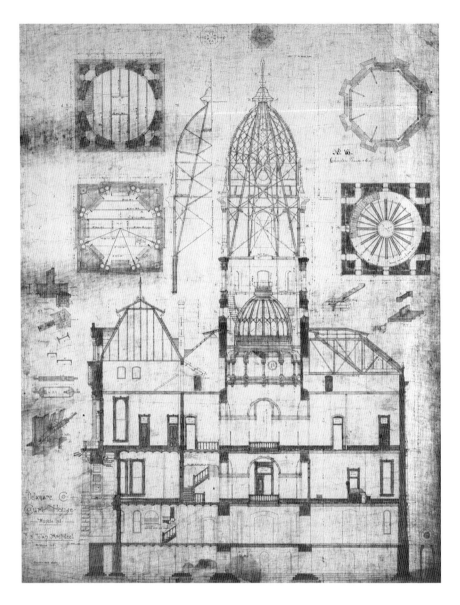

Landers as a stonecutter to help carve the courthouse's sandstone blocks around 1884. When Landers wasn't cutting stone, he worked as a general laborer on construction projects around town. The discovery of natural gas brought tremendous wealth to Muncie. New buildings went up all over the city. Skilled labor was in high demand.

Landers did so well that he purchased an acre of property near the Delaware County Fair Grounds sometime around 1890. However, the Panic

Opposite: The 1885 plans for the third Delaware County Courthouse. *Courtesy of Ball State University Libraries' Bracken Archive and Special Collections.*

Above: The ornate third Delaware County Courthouse, early twentieth century. *Courtesy of the Delaware County Historical Society, Mike Mavis Collection.*

Right: The Delaware County Courthouse, circa 1966. Landers carved some of this. *Courtesy of Ball State University Libraries' Bracken Archive and Special Collections.*

Workers dismantling the second Delaware County Courthouse in 1884. *Courtesy of the Delaware County Historical Society, Mike Mavis Collection.*

of 1893 left the old stonecutter destitute. Landers moved in with his friend August Schaubhut at the Hodge Block on the southwest corner of High and Main Streets. Schaubhut, a former Muncie volunteer fireman, was listed in the city's 1893–94 *Emerson City Directory* as a "tailor, scourer and repairer."[190]

About nine months after Landers's ghost appeared to the Selma ice hauler, the *Herald* wrote a follow-up article accusing Schaubhut and Landers of making counterfeit money. "There is one man in Muncie," the *Herald* wrote, "who was intimately acquainted with Landers over a year ago when he had a room in the Hodge block. This man says Landers was a counterfeiter."[191] The informant discovered him once "engaged in making bogus money." Apparently, he had a half-dollar mold and was minting fake currency out of ordinary metal.

At some point in early 1896, Schaubhut became deathly ill, but Landers stayed and took care of him. The situation grew so bad that "Schaubhut was taken to the county infirmary," and Landers went with him.[192] Schaubhut didn't last long and died on May 9. He was buried at Beech Grove Cemetery.

Landers, however, stayed at the county infirmary as a resident, perhaps because he had no place else to go. Superintendent Strawder Watson described him as "a very bad man to get along with and caused a great deal of trouble on account of his temper."[193]

In late May or early June 1896, Landers met Jesse Brown, a new infirmary resident. Brown was seventy-six years old, without a "single tooth and his hearing is slightly affected."[194] Brown had settled in Muncietown around 1844 and worked as a teamster. Then, in the 1850s, he managed the livery stable at the popular Jo Davis House on the southeast corner of Main and Walnut Streets.

Brown and Landers became fast friends. Three weeks before the stonecutter's mangled corpse was found on Selma Pike, the duo left the infirmary to peddle miracle salves around east-central Indiana. Their ointment was "purported to cure rheumatism and a hundred other diseases."[195] They traveled extensively through Muncie, Marion, Jonesboro, Gas City and Wheeling. A few days before his death, Landers was in Alexandria, where he bought a one-eyed horse and a dog.

Delaware County Asylum, circa 1890s. *Courtesy of Ball State University Libraries' Bracken Archive and Special Collections.*

The salve peddlers returned to Muncie on July 6 and camped somewhere in the Whitely neighborhood. On Tuesday, the duo made their way to Heekin Park on Muncie's southside for a leisurely afternoon. The two were spotted "sitting on a log smoking their pipes."[196] A Munsonian by the name of William Vailes stopped and chatted with the pair for "over an hour on different subjects, and during the conversation the one.…Landers, showed him a revolver and watch chain which he wanted to sell, but Vailes did not buy them."[197]

Muncie Police, who still suspected foul play, arrested Jesse Brown at his nephew's house on South Grant Street. He was questioned extensively about Lander's death. Apparently, the two had gotten into a fight at Heekin over provisions. Brown left to go buy something, and when he returned, his stuff was piled by a tree. Landers had left the park, abandoning his friend. Brown reluctantly gathered his meager belongings and went to stay at his nephew's house. The two went out drinking at the White Swan Saloon around 9:30 p.m. and then returned home and went to sleep.

The cops didn't have any actual evidence to hold Brown for murder. Plus, the tired, homeless, seventy-six-year-old man without teeth didn't really strike anyone as capable of such brutal violence. Muncie Police held Brown for a few days on the spurious charge of stealing an infirmary jacket. As for the old stonecutter, he was last seen alive buying tobacco from Schull's Grocery in Selma on the evening of July 7.

Two competing theories emerged as to how Landers died. Sheriff William Sherry thought Landers was murdered. He believed that a fight had ensued at the infirmary's gate, where an unknown assailant hit the stonecutter over the head with a blunt object. Landers then ran to the fence and tried to climb it but was hit again and passed out. Whoever—or whatever—was attacking Landers then tied him to the back of the wagon and dragged him down Selma Pike until his death.

The competing theory was offered by Muncie Police patrolman William McIlvaine, who thought that the stonecutter died from a terrible accident. McIlvaine believed that Landers, a heavy smoker, had returned to the infirmary late evening to enjoy a puff by the big hickory tree out front. There he was suddenly attacked by a coughing spasm and hacked up blood by the tree and fence. "Knowing that he was in a serious condition, he got into his wagon and started to Muncie to see a doctor. He became so weak that he fell from the seat with his head against the wheel," got caught and was pulled under.[198] He was dragged down the gravel pike for two miles before breaking loose. The horse, relieved of her burden, eventually made its

The second Delaware County Infirmary, circa 1900. *Courtesy of Jeff Koenker.*

way back to Muncie going in the same direction. McIlvaine's theory, though plausible, didn't consider Lander's dog with the cut eye.

The same day Lander's ghost appeared to the ice hauler from Selma, the *Herald* reported that the county had auctioned off all his belongings for a measly $4.35 ($160 in 2024 dollars). The horse was sold to John Stanley for $2, the wagon to Will Wood for $1 and the harness to George Shaw for $0.50.[199] All charges were dropped against Jesse Brown on July 18.

The cause of Landers's death was never determined. His ghost was (probably) never seen again.

CHAPTER 7

YORKTOWN'S HEADLESS SPECTER

On All Souls' Day in 1901, the *Indianapolis News* published an odd article about a haunted farmhouse southwest of Yorktown in rural Mount Pleasant Township.[200] The story was written by William Blodgett after the veteran reporter spent a night in the house with a friend identified only as "Dick."

The duo decided to brave an overnight stay after learning about a "house up near Yorktown with an uncanny story connected with it." The story that reached Indy told of a man who "shot himself and cut his throat in the house a good many years ago, and ever since the house has had a ghostly visitor and all kinds of funny things have happened, according to the country folk thereabouts."[201] The spirit also appeared as a "headless horseman, taking the shape of a dim, gigantic ghost" that galloped "about the barn lot and prance along the road until he disappears in misty nothingness."[202]

Blodgett described the house as an "old-time country" place, at least a half century old. "It was located on the National road, a mile or so from the village of Yorktown, about three and a half miles from Daleville." Blodgett didn't mean *the* National Road, what we now call U.S. 40, but rather the old federal government road that ran through Muncie, Yorktown and Daleville. Today, we know this route as Indiana State Road 32, but locals in 1901 commonly called it "Yorktown Pike" or the "Indianapolis Road."

Once in Yorktown, Blodgett and Dick were greeted warmly by the haunted house's live inhabitants: Charles Augustas "Gus" Burgess; his wife, Mollie; and their six-year-old son, Harold. According to Blodgett, Gus Burgess was

TALE ᴏꜰ ᴀ HOOSIER HAUNTED HOUSE

HAUNTED HOUSE 'ROUND WHICH THE HEADLESS HORSEMAN RIDES.

Top: The story's headline in the *Indianapolis News*, November 2, 1901. *Courtesy Hoosier State Chronicles*.

Bottom: Gus Burgess's haunted farmhouse as it appeared in the *Indianapolis News*, November 2, 1901. *Courtesy Hoosier State Chronicles*.

"glad to have the ghost investigated. We were welcomed to the house and Mrs. Burgess smiled when she learned our errand. She had met many such visitors before."[203]

The Burgess farmhouse stood "back from the road only a little distance, and is partly hidden by a small grove of locust trees that cast silhouettes of twisted shapes on the white, moonlit highway."[204] Blodgett felt that the "whole place seemed to be cut off from the outer world by an invisible wall. The farm of 160 splendid acres is situated in what is called the Kilgore neighborhood a half mile, perhaps, from the Pike's Peak school-house."[205]

RES. OF THE LATE DAVID KILGORE, M.T. PLEASANT TP. DELAWARE CO. IND.

Blodgett didn't provide an exact address, but his description of the farmhouse's immediate surroundings provides us with an approximate location. The "Kilgore neighborhood" was in reference to farms owned or managed by the descendants of David Kilgore, a prominent early Delaware County lawyer and politician. In his prime, Kilgore owned huge tracts of land in west Mount Pleasant Township. After he died in 1879, the Kilgore estate was divided among heirs and sold away within a few generations. But in 1901, several of his children and grandchildren still owned farms west of Yorktown, including Alfred, Charles, Clarence and Obediah.

The Pike's Peak schoolhouse Blodgett referenced was known officially as Salem Township School No. 2. It was one of several schoolhouses in the immediate area.[206] The "Kilgore School," or Mount Pleasant Township School No. 9, was just south of the Burgess farm. In the 1880s, Gus and his brother Clyde Burgess attended another area schoolhouse, a one-story brick school known as Reed, or Mount Pleasant Township School No. 6.[207]

In a trope far older than Stephen King, Blodgett also made a point to mention an "Indian graveyard" near the farm. "Even to this day," the reporter told Indianapolis readers, "bones, arrows and crude implements of the chase are plowed up."

He also began his article by briefly recounting a bogus "Legend of an Indiana Treasure."[208] The folktale, which was surely told to him by local Yorktowners, had it that a Native American village once existed nearby on what became David Kilgore's farm. The village chief was Wasaheto, better known as "the Fox." Wasaheto died unexpectedly on a hunting trip

Opposite: Engraving of the Kilgore Farm from Thomas Helm's *History of Delaware County* (1881). *Courtesy of the Delaware County Historical Society*.

Left: David Kilgore from Thomas Helm's *History of Delaware County* (1881). *Courtesy of the Delaware County Historical Society.*

not long after he buried $5,000 in gold. Unfortunately, he hadn't shared the whereabouts of his treasure before dying.

Some of the locals believed this story and occasionally dug around the area looking for gold. They grew tired one year of the fruitless searches and hired a clairvoyant to assist in locating the hoard. During a séance led by a "wonderful medium," they learned that "the money had been buried by The Fox at a point where the White river used to run close to a great rock." Every now and again, "even to this day, men with spades, shovels and picks, dig great holes in the old river bank looking for buried treasure." But no one ever found anything.

No part of this "legend" is true, except that there really was a Native American village nearby. However, it existed before David Kilgore and his heirs arrived in what is now Delaware County.

The Lenape Native American village of Owenachki existed just west of what is now Yorktown from approximately 1796 until 1812. The small community was likely on the south side of the river, about where Priest Ford Road meets State Road 32 today.[209] Owenachki's titular chief was Hockingpomsga, at least through the year 1809.[210]

White River Lenape were rich in many things in the early 1800s, but gold wasn't one of them. Archaeologists in the late twentieth century found artifacts at the site, although they dated to a much earlier period of Native American history—hundreds if not thousands of years before Lenape people or Kilgores lived along the river.[211]

I should also note that the Lenape word for fox in the Unami language is *òkwës*[212] and, in Munsee, *waaluwees*.[213] The Myaamia (Miami) word for fox is *paapankamwa*.[214] If "Wasaheto" and the bit about "buried Indian treasure" seems like a stupid story made up by white people, that's because it was.

Despite the legend's nonsense, the real Lenape village of Owenachki existed in what became the "Kilgore Neighborhood" in Mount Pleasant Township. Anyone living and, more importantly, farming the area in the mid-1800s would have uncovered remnants of human habitation. Stories about such finds surely passed down to children and grandchildren, many of whom still lived in Yorktown at the turn of the century.

By the time Blodgett stayed on the haunted Burgess Farm in October 1901, the area below the long-abandoned Owenachki site had become a wetlands. He wrote that nearby "is a boggy swamp where cattle sometimes mire and snakes and other slimy things abide. Here it is thought that the Headless Horseman saddles his steed, and every Tuesday night, goes on his nocturnal ride."[215]

Not long after the reporters arrived, Burgess took Blodgett and Dick on a tour of the property. The trek around the old farm provided ample time for Burgess to weave his haunted yarn:

Cyrus Slack was a country physician who lived in this house about twenty-five years ago. He was a famous doctor in his day and used to travel all over this country healing the sick, and he accumulated a good deal of money… as he grew in years, his mind became unsettled and one night he went out into the yard and shot himself. The wound did not kill him, and with the blood pouring from his body, he went into the house, up the stairs to a little room in the northwest corner and cut his throat. The blood from this second wound ate into the floor and the stain is still here and so are the marks of his boot heels where he staggered against the wall. But he did not die there. His death came at some hospital. The supposition is that he has returned in spirit, if not in body.[216]

Burgess related how "strange things have happened since we have lived here, now more than six years.…I have heard groans coming from that room up-stairs, and I have heard things rolling over the floor and the sound of music, just like someone was playing the violin."

Burgess and his family also heard:

> people laugh and foot-falls on the stairs as if someone were coming down, but no one ever appeared. The door between the dining-room and the kitchen swings open at all hours and without any apparent reason. There is a little cupboard out in the kitchen where the old doctor kept his medicines, and the door to that kept swinging open until I took it off the hinges. [217]

It's possible that Blodgett made all this up, but I'm inclined to believe that he was reporting the story as told to him by Burgess and anyone else he interviewed in Yorktown. There are *some* truthful elements in the tale, but a little historical investigation reveals a hodgepodge assortment of unrelated facts, woven together as a ghost story.

I looked extensively for a Cyrus Slack in the historical records but couldn't find anyone with that name living in Mount Pleasant Township. The only contemporary doctor with the surname Slack was George Washington Slack, a well-known nineteenth-century Yorktown physician. [218] Although born in Buck County, Pennsylvania, in 1825, Slack spent most of his life in Mount Pleasant Township after moving here with family in 1837. After graduating from Chicago's Rush Medical School in 1854, he returned to Delaware County and opened a family practice in Yorktown.

Sometime around the Civil War, Slack inherited his family's farm in Section 21 of Mount Pleasant Township—just east of Yorktown along the White River. [219] The farm grew over the years, expanding into Section 20 next to Obediah Kilgore's sprawling estate. Slack also owned a few acres along Yorktown's western border. The property had a building on it nicknamed the "Old Martin Box." [220]

George W. Slack appeared a few times in local papers in the late nineteenth century. In May 1880, the *Muncie Daily Times* wrote that Dr. Slack "continues to practice medicine and farming." Slack said that he "farms for pleasure and doctors for a living." [221] Later in October, Slack is mentioned in an article as having provided medical attention to William Erther. The young farmer was crushed in an accident nearby, and Slack was solicited for aid. Erther survived his injuries thanks to Dr. Slack's quick response.

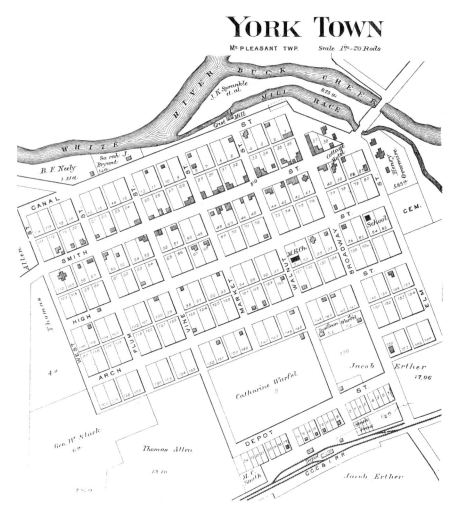

Above: The town of Yorktown from the 1887 *Atlas of Delaware County*. *Courtesy of the Delaware County Historical Society.*

Opposite: The "Kilgore Neighborhood" west of Yorktown in Mount Pleasant Township, from the 1887 *Atlas of Delaware County*. *Courtesy of the Delaware County Historical Society.*

Three years later, in August 1883, Dr. Slack was again pressed into emergency service when he treated the stab wounds of a fellow Yorktown physician, J.H. Shively. He received the injury when making a routine house call to treat a woman identified only as "Mrs. Sears."[222] Sears was boarding with her husband at Obediah Kilgore's farmhouse down the road from Slack's place.

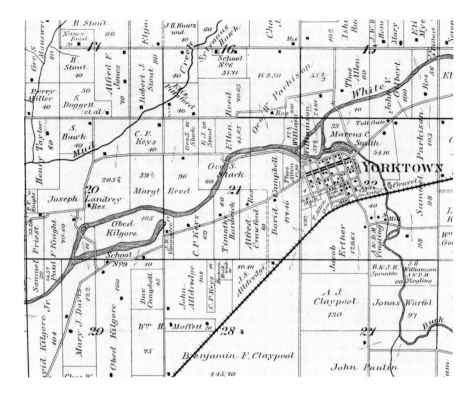

After attending to Mrs. Sears, Shively was invited for dinner and sat down at the kitchen table to dine with the rest of the house. Welcoming travelers to a common meal was a neighborly custom at the time, especially at boardinghouses. As everyone sat to eat, "Mr. Kilgore, who had been lying down in his bedroom, came out." At that point, the *Morning News* braced readers, "the stories differ."[223]

According to Shively, he shook hands with Obed as he sat down at the table. Old man Kilgore "asked his wife for whiskey and drank a little remaining in a half pint flask and sent Mr. Sears out for another." Kilgore's demeanor then abruptly changed. He looked menacingly at Shively and lunged at him, shouting "to get out of his house as he struck him, cutting him over the heart."[224]

Obed Kilgore's version wasn't exactly exonerating. Kilgore said that when he saw Shively at the table, he yelled, "There is that god damned doctor again." He ordered Shively to leave "five or six times before he began striking him, and that Shively had plenty of time to escape."

Kilgore's mother-in-law said that the fight had started after Shively criticized Kilgore's excessive drinking. Indeed, the *News* concluded, "whiskey came very near furnishing another victim again yesterday to death who stalks throughout our land hand in hand with his agent Rum, seeking whom he may devour. This time it was near Yorktown and again Mr. Obediah Kilgore was selected as the medium through which the vile fluid, the destroyer of much happiness, should act."[225]

Shively ran out the house, followed by a very drunk Kilgore, who chased him down the drive with a shotgun, "threatening to shoot him." At the front gate, old Obediah just sat down and "ate his dinner with the weapon across his lap."

Shively "drove to Slack's where his wound was probed and dressed." He made a full recovery thanks to the doctor's good care. Prosecutors sympathetic to his alcoholism later dropped attempted murder charges after Kilgore pleaded guilty to assault and battery.

In all cases, Dr. George Washington Slack appears in the historical record as an upstanding citizen, someone well respected in Yorktown and known throughout Delaware County as a reliable physician. He died on January 10, 1886, but not of suicide. The *Indianapolis Journal* reported a day later that "Dr. Geo. W. Slack, one of the oldest and most prominent physicians of this place, died very suddenly, at 9:20 o'clock this morning, of paralysis of the heart, aged sixty years."[226] The *Huntington Democrat* lamented that "James R. Slack and mother, Mrs. A.P. Slack, of this city, were called to Yorktown, Ind., Monday to attend the funeral of Dr. Washington Slack whose death from apoplexy had occurred the day previous."[227] Slack died of either a stroke or heart attack.

Fifteen years later, Gus Burgess's incredulous story of "Cyrus" Slack's violent suicide was fiction. I suspect that because Burgess lived on or near the doctor's farm, a character with the surname Slack gave the story a measure of local credibility.

However, in keeping within the general spirit of this book, Burgess's encounter with the supernatural shouldn't be dismissed outright because he concocted part of the story. The particulars of his narrative, fictional or not, hint at some very real fears that existed in Mount Pleasant Township at the time.

A farmer living east of Muncie had died of suicide the year before in April 1900. The *Times* reported that "ill health and business troubles caused Cyrus Wilkinson, 43, to kill himself Saturday noon at his home, two miles east of Muncie."[228] After downing a bottle of carbolic acid, Cyrus was found in the barn unconscious by his wife. He was carried inside the farmhouse and promptly died.

A handwritten note from Dr. George Slack asking township trustees for poor relief. *Courtesy of Ball State University Libraries' Bracken Archive and Special Collections.*

The papers claimed that Wilkinson was distraught over being sued by Anna Eiler, the farm's owner. After several missed rent payments, Eiler was attempting to evict the Wilkinsons in court, despite the family having farmed the property for years.[229]

The *Star* reminded readers that Wilkinson was once a murder suspect. "The deceased is the Cyrus Wilkinson arrested in connection with the murder of William Stoll in Muncie about two years ago."[230] At the time, Wilkinson was released a few days later because police didn't have sufficient evidence to hold him. The *News* wrote that Wilkinson was "regarded as a peaceable man with none of the traits on his face showing him to be a person with such a heart as would be required to execute" a murder.[231]

In the spring of 1900, residents across Delaware County became alarmed at Cyrus Wilkinson's suicide—not only at the manner but also because "Wilkinson's death makes the fifth death by suicide in the county within six days and the seventh attempt at suicide."[232]

CYRUS WILKINSON.

Sketch of Cyrus Wilkinson in the *Muncie Daily Herald*, September 13, 1898. *Scanned from microfilm at Ball State University's Bracken Library.*

By May 8, six residents had died of suicide in the preceding five-week span.[233] The lost included John Ehrman, a retired farmer who lived on a small estate between Yorktown and Daleville. Despairing over poor health, Ehrman cut his own throat on April 23. The *Muncie Daily Herald* wrote that "John Ehrman of Daleville, was one of Delaware county's oldest citizens and was well known in the community in which he lived." Ehrman's "act is considered by his family and friends to have been due to despondency and poor health."[234]

Later in July 1900, a sixty-five-year-old Yorktown tanner and former gas company president named Henry Overmire attempted suicide but survived. On the morning of July 26, Overmire walked down to the Buck Creek from his house with a loaded .32-caliber revolver. He fired several shots into his head, all of which entered his skull, but none killed him. The *Times* wrote that "both balls tore through the brain destroying the ears."[235] Hearing the shots, his wife called for help.

Neighbors found Overmire lying in the creek, "with blood flowing from the wounds made by the bullets." He was taken to Dr. J.R. Downing's in Yorktown, who called in an assist from Dr. William H. Kemper of Muncie. The doctors informed "the family that there were practically no hopes."[236]

Luckily for Henry Overmire, the doctors were wrong. He survived and, a week later, regained consciousness and recovered in Muncie. The *Times* wrote that "notwithstanding the fact that bullets are yet in the brain he still lives and even bids fair to recover." The paper concluded that "if Overmire

Yorktown Man Dies

Henry Overmire.

Henry Overmire, from the *Muncie Morning Star,* January 8, 1912. *Scanned from microfilm at Ball State University's Bracken Library.*

should defy fate and recover, as now seems entirely probable, it will be almost a miracle."[237]

On August 7, the *Morning Star* wrote that Overmire is "rapidly gaining in strength and is sure to live now." The report is even more remarkable because it noted that Overmire had shot himself *five* times in the head. Doctors later discovered new wounds on his skull that were healing. They managed to remove two bullets, but the remaining three were forever "imbedded in the brain or flesh."[238]

Overmire would go on to live another decade, dying of Bright's disease at the age of seventy-four in January 1912. He was remembered in the *Morning Star* as "a pioneer resident of Yorktown."

Growing up west of Yorktown, Gus Burgess surely knew these very real stories of well-known doctors and settlers. Perhaps he interweaved bits and pieces to embellish his own ghostly tale—elements possibly designed to frighten his already traumatized neighbors. In the very least, the previous year's suicides left families mourning and on edge—haunted, one might say, by ghosts eerily similar to Cyrus Slack.

Burgess also claimed that two people had tried and failed to live in the old Slack farmhouse, but the specter scared them away. On the tour of the house, Burgess remarked to Blodgett that one of them "saw the ghost right in this room and he shot at it a number of times. See, here are the bullet holes." Burgess proceeded to point out several holes in the wall.

"Sure enough," Blodgett wrote, "the bullet holes were in the woodwork, showing that someone had been indulging in pistol practice at short range."[239]

In the room where Cyrus Slack supposedly cut his throat, Blodgett noted a dark stain "as if a sudden flow of blood had struck the floor and then run several feet, making a long, ragged ribbon. It had every appearance of blood turned from its fresh color by age. Across the room, close to the grimy wall, was the mark of two boot heels."[240]

"That," said Burgess, "is where he is supposed to have stood just after he cut his throat and tracked the blood from the other spot."[241] Despite every attempt from Gus and Mollie to remove the stain, it remained as a dark daily reminder of what happened.

On the way downstairs, Blodgett asked about the Headless Horseman. "Did you ever see him?"

"A number of times," Burgess said. "I have shot at him often, but I have never been able to hit him. He rides a sort of a dark horse, just like the doctor used to ride, and he is sort of thin and misty like, and has no head."[242]

The decapitated ghost rider started his haunt at the barn and rode out to the road. "Sometimes he just seems to bob up out of the ground, and lots of people have had their horses shy at him and he has ridden around people who were driving along the road."

Burgess continued:

HUNTING FOR THE BLOOD STAINS.

Blodgett looking for the blood of Cyrus Slack. From the *Indianapolis News*, November 2, 1901. *Courtesy of Hoosier State Chronicles.*

> *When Bill Fuquay lived here he always had trouble to get his horses into the barn after night. They would snort and tremble and seem very much afraid, and if Bill got home late he would never go into the barn after night. The doors would be fastened sometimes, too, and Bill could hardly get them open, and then at other times the doors would fly open and Bill could not get them shut. But the part of the barn where the doctor used to keep his horse is pulled down now and the Headless Horseman just comes up from the ground.*[243]

After walking through the house, Blodgett and his friend Dick "went out in the air and wandered over the farm and down to the boggy swamp and stood on the rock under which the old Indian is supposed to have buried the gold." The pair noticed many "excavations by those who had faith in the medium to dig for money."[244]

Blodgett surmised that "there is no question but the people in the neighborhood are firmly convinced that there is a supernatural something about the house, and there are people who will not drive by it on a dark night."

Both Dick and William Blodgett returned to the Burgess farmhouse and spent the night. They slept soundly until Dick woke up in a panic, gurgling and calling for help. Blodgett shouted, "What is the matter?"

THE HEADLESS HORSEMAN.

A SPECTER THAT HAS OUTLIVED GENERATIONS.

LEGEND OF THE INDIANS

News Men Sleep a Night in the Haunted House—a Bloody Tragedy Recalled—The Experiences of a Night.

Left: The headless ghost rides west of Yorktown. From the *Indianapolis News*, November 2, 1901. *Courtesy of Hoosier State Chronicles.*

Below: A rendering of the headless ghost. From the *Indianapolis News*, November 2, 1901. *Courtesy of Hoosier State Chronicles.*

Dick croaked back, "I thought a ghost without a head on a headless horse was chasing me and made me jump over a high cliff, and just as I struck a fellow all in white was trying to crowd three fingers down my throat." Dick was having a nightmare.

Alas, that was the only disturbance. "If there are ghosts in the Burgess home," Blodgett told Indianapolis readers, "they were taking a rest last Tuesday night." The pair returned to Indy the next morning via the Interurban to report their harrowing tale.

Above: Blodgett's traveling companion had a nightmare. From the *Indianapolis News*, November 2, 1901. *Courtesy of Hoosier State Chronicles.*

Left: An ad to stay on the Burgess Farm. From the *Indianapolis News*, November 11, 1901. *Courtesy of Hoosier State Chronicles.*

Opposite: Mollie, Harold and Gus Burgess. From the *Indianapolis News*, November 2, 1901. *Courtesy of Hoosier State Chronicles.*

GUS BURGESS, HIS WIFE AND CHILD, TENANTS OF THE HAUNTED HOUSE.

Other than the modern retellings of this story, I can't find any other contemporary accounts of the Burgess Farm haunting beyond the 1901 *Indianapolis News* story. About a week after this article was published, a curious advertisement appeared in the *Indianapolis News*, boldly proclaiming, "Five dollars for spending a night in the haunted house." Readers learned that "Gus Burgess, who lives in the haunted house recently told of in The News, offers $5 to any person who will remain all night in the room in which Dr. Slack cut his throat." Two boys from Daleville, identified only as Cornelius and Wigner, decided to "accept the offer."[245]

Burgess went on to become a respected member in his community. In addition to maintaining the farm, he served as Yorktown's postmaster in the 1920s and as town marshal during the Second World War. He died in March 1963 at the age of eighty-six. His obit said nothing about the haunting.[246]

Whatever was lurking around his farm in 1901 remained at Burgess's death, as it does now, a total mystery.

Chapter 8

Hoaxed on the Whitney Viaduct

Some hauntings in Delaware County had very human origins, even if decades passed before anyone learned the truth. One such apparition occurred in mid-April 1930 when a ghost began appearing nightly on the Whitney Road viaduct, just east of Muncie in Liberty Township.

Today, we know it as South County Road 475 East, but in 1930, the north–south route was known as Whitney Road. The thoroughfare connected the old Muncie and Smithfield Pike (Inlow Springs Road) with Selma Pike (State Road 32). A viaduct bridge was completed in 1924 to carry Whitney Road over the New York Central Railroad tracks (CSX).[247]

On April 12, the *Muncie Morning Star* reported that "consistent rumors of a ghost that hovers about the viaduct near the county infirmary, four miles east of Muncie on the road to Selma, has proven too much for residents of Muncie and surrounding cities."[248] The *Star* quoted an unnamed eyewitness of the ghost as saying, "It comes from under the viaduct every night between 11 and 12 o'clock and floats about the railroad track. It makes no noise, merely floats about and finally disappears."[249]

At first, dozens of people started driving out nightly to see the spirit. Any given midnight, "there may be seen from twenty to fifty carloads of persons parked near the viaduct, anxiously and expectantly awaiting the appearance of the apparition."[250] Traffic was so bad on the bridge that the MPD dispatched an officer to keep the roads around the viaduct clear for safe passage.

Above: The Whitney Viaduct in 1966, taken by Dick Greene. *Courtesy of Ball State University Libraries' Bracken Archive and Special Collections.*

Opposite: The 1936 map showing the Whitney Viaduct over the Big Four/New York Central tracks. *Courtesy of the Indiana State Library.*

The city's movie theaters, perhaps worried that the spook was stealing patrons, took out a humorous ad in the *Evening Press*. It read, "If you are going out to see the Ghost tonight, take a box of Pop Corn along; you'll enjoy it! Take a BIG box, maybe the GHOST would like some—EVERY BODY ELSE DOES. Get It at the Liberty or Royal Theaters."[251]

If you'll recall, a haunting once happened near this same location in 1896 when the ghost of Joe Landers appeared to a Selma ice hauler. Whitney Road ends at Selma Pike, immediately south of the Delaware County Infirmary.

It's unclear if anyone in April 1930 remembered Landers, but soon hundreds of people were nightly visiting the Whitney Road viaduct to catch a glimpse of this new ghost. A story circulated that the specter "jumps from the bridge to a Big Four passenger train."[252] The explanation was perhaps given because the ghost only ever appeared on nights when trains were oncoming, heading east from Muncie.

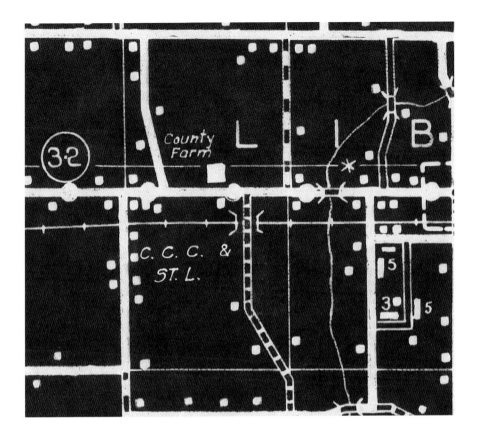

The cops at first thought that the spirit might be an infirmary resident roaming around at night. The inmates, as they were often called, wore white pajamas to sleep. If an infirmary resident had been walking over the bridge, they might have been mistaken for something beyond the grave in headlights. However, a staff "checkup on the inmates revealed none of them had ever been missing between the hours" in question.[253]

The ghost stopped appearing as soon as the press picked up the story, although large crowds continued to gather on the Whitney Viaduct. On April 14, the *Star* wrote that no fewer than two hundred automobiles had parked along the bridge, but the ghost "failed to walk last night."[254] The ghost watchers were disappointed, as you can imagine, and "intimated that unless performances are more regular, they will refuse to credence the story which has lured motorists to the bridge for the past week."[255]

The police abandoned the "escaped infirmary inmate" theory and instead believed that the haunting was caused by an optical illusion, hypothesizing that the ghost was "either the shadow of the locomotive

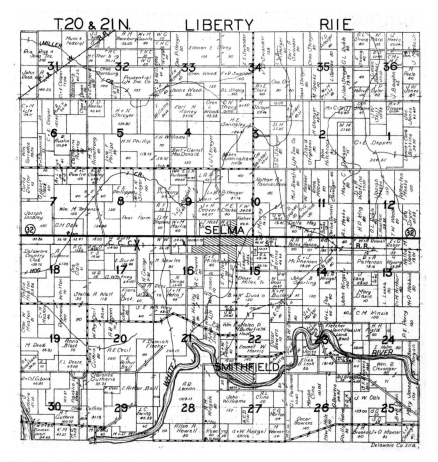

The "X" in Section 17 on the map marks the spot of the Viaduct Bridge. Image is taken from a 1930 Delaware County plat map of Liberty Township. *Courtesy of the Indiana State Library.*

head-light on telegraph wires under the bridge or a will-o-the-wisp mixed with imagination."[256]

People kept coming by the hundreds as April waned. The *Muncie Evening Press* joked that the ghost "should prove a money maker for some ambitious promoter able to get an option on all the available parking in the vicinity."[257] A reporter on the scene overheard one ghost watcher say to a friend, "I'm going to be back here tomorrow night, damaged fenders and mud holes notwithstanding."[258] Locals grew rightly irritated at all the traffic.

The situation became untenable. On the night of Sunday, April 27, Delaware County sheriff Fred Puckett and his deputies descended on the scene like Valkyries. They cleared traffic and "accumulated a list of the

Sheriff Fred Puckett, ghostbuster. *Courtesy of Ball State University Libraries' Bracken Archive and Special Collections.*

The writer and historian Dick Greene in about 1980. *Courtesy of the Delaware County Historical Society, Mike Mavis Collection.*

license numbers of machines that jammed the roadway."[259] If ghost watching returned to the Whitney Road viaduct after Sheriff Puckett's blitz, it was never reported in local papers.

The story became a part of eastern Delaware County lore in ensuing decades—a fading tale told in the backdrop of the Great Depression and the Second World War. But locals did remember it.

In his article about the viaduct haunting twenty years later in July 1950, *Muncie Star* columnist and historian Dick Greene recalled "rather vaguely a tale that went the rounds some years ago and caused people to trek in numbers to that overhead." Greene remembered that "some person of keen sight or keener imagination" had drawn crowds after "seeing a ghost in the neighborhood."

"Maybe it was a trainman," Green speculated. "It might have been a motorist or a pedestrian who reported this spectral figure, or something equally gossamer. I never did get the straight of it, and, for that matter, I'm wondering whether anyone else did."[260]

Greene was writing in his "Seen and Heard in Our Neighborhood" column, a feature in the *Muncie Star* published during the latter half of the twentieth century. His articles dealt in folklore, local history, culture and little bits of the everyday. He was a veteran reporter and well known in Muncie as a public historian. Greene knew much about the city and the surrounding area and often interacted with readers through his column.

Sure enough, someone took his bait of "I'm wondering whether anyone else did." In his August 9, 1950 column, Greene wrote that "it was all a prank, or a gag, and involved several young men, one of whom tells the story but prefers to be anonymous."[261] The nameless prankster recounted the ghostly details to Greene:

One of us had read something in a magazine about cutting out a human figure in silhouette, pasting it on a looking glass and then using the glass as a reflector…we took a small mirror. Oh, big enough to hang on a wall but still small enough to be slipped under a raincoat and carried without being noticed. A human figure was cut out of the black paper and was pasted on the mirror…we had been told that if a light were thrown on the mirror fixed this way it would show the figure which would look mighty odd. We got in a barn loft, held the glass while someone drove a car toward us. We reflected the beam of light. The others said it looked very odd. Like a ghost.[262]

After a successful first test, the mischief makers went down to the Whitney Road viaduct one evening and stood on the bridge. When a train came,

An 1864 *Harper's* illustration of a "ghost" trick, similar to that used on the Whitney Viaduct. *Courtesy of Wikimedia.*

the mirror with the cutout silhouette would "catch the headlight beam in the glass and reflect the ghostly figure."[263] Greene's anonymous informant didn't know how the word got out, "but before long people were coming in numbers to the overhead to see the 'ghost.' We worked it pretty carefully."[264]

On the nights in question, one kid stood on the bridge, closely flanked by his co-conspirators hiding the mirror. Two more miscreants went down below the bridge to stand with the crowd by the tracks to wait for the ghost. When a late New York Central train came from Muncie, its front headlight hit the mirror and bounced back a ghostly image. At the right moment, one of the pranksters would yell, "There's a ghost!" or "There it is!"

"Now when you come to see a thing like that," the prankster said, "your imagination already is keyed up and when it goes to work, you really see things."[265]

The gang perfected their ghostly hauntings, continuing it for several nights. "We had to go to the bridge early in order to get the spot in the center." However, within a few days "there were people along the tracks and the road and so many cars that we thought the conditions were dangerous. So we just quit. And that was the 'ghost.'"[266]

Knowing that it was a prank, of course, takes the enigma out of the haunting. But this story does reveal the extent to which people wanted to connect with the supernatural. Perhaps we all just want to witness something out of this world. The unnamed prankster concluded much the same to Dick Greene in 1950: "People were fooled or maybe they weren't, but anyhow many of them did see something."[267]

CHAPTER 9

BLY AND THE PHANTOM AIR RAID

E very Friday morning at 11:00 a.m. sharp, Delaware County's Emergency Management Agency tests the outdoor warning sirens. For a few seconds, ominous shrills blast across every corner of Greater Muncie in chilling unison. In the forty-four years I've lived here, they only ever blare during Friday tests and tornado warnings. The sirens are a necessary but grim reminder that unexpected terror might descend from the skies any moment.

The sirens date to the Second World War, when a fear existed that German or Japanese war planes would bomb American cities with defense manufacturing. Enemy bombers weren't ever likely to appear in the skies above Muncie in the 1940s, but the city participated in air-raid testing as part of a coordinated nationwide civilian defense effort.

After the United States entered the war in late 1941, most Munsonians did their part to help. Local factories spent 1942 retooling to meet U.S. Department of War orders. Thousands of Delaware County residents enlisted or were drafted that year, and Victory Gardens popped up across the city. By year's end, rationing had taken hold of daily life. Homefront security was provided by the Civil Defense Corps. The CDC also built and tested Muncie's air-raid warning system.

The first test was performed at GM's Chevy plant in Avondale on September 8, 1942. Archie McCabe, the city's fire chief at the time, organized the demonstration to determine if the siren would meet city needs.[268] Similar tests happened all over the United States. In northern Indiana, thirteen cities planned an air-raid test mid-September, coordinated by the U.S. Army and local civilian defense leaders.[269]

Despite McCabe's success with the siren, a city-wide system couldn't be installed in time for the CDC's planned air-raid tests that fall. Factory whistles instead served as signals. Muncie's first coordinated whistle test occurred on Monday, November 23, 1942. The *Muncie Star* reported that "Ball Brothers, Broderick Company, Chevrolet-Muncie, Ontario Manufacturing Company, Muncie Malleable, Indiana Bridge, Delco-Remy, Indiana Steel and Wire, Kuhners, Muncie Foundry, Owens-Illinois, and Warner Gear" all participated.[270]

With the factory whistle warning system tested and ready, Muncie's Civil Defense Corps planned a larger "dim-out" test on Sunday, November 29, 1942. A dim-out mixed a "shelter in place" drill with a partial blackout and traffic restrictions. Every Munsonian except first responders were expected to go indoors and stay for a half hour with all lights off. Factories, churches and businesses were also all required to go black. However, since it was just a dim-out, street and railroad lights remained on, as they did at Ball Memorial Hospital. Air-raid wardens patrolled city streets in specified districts to ensure compliance and to relay ground conditions back to CDC's central command.

At precisely 10:00 p.m., all of Muncie's factories blew their whistles in a coordinated pattern. The city slowed to a total halt. Emergency personnel made test runs, while a spotter in the Civil Air Patrol flew overhead taking notes on what factories might remain visible to enemy bombers.[271]

The test was hailed as an "outstanding success."[272] The *Star* reported that "the city of Muncie, a bright corner of Hoosierdom since natural gas flambeaus cast their reflection in the mud puddles of unpaved uptown streets, turned down the lights last night in its first wartime trial dim-out."[273]

The success prompted the CDC to plan a total blackout drill. A blackout required *all* lights switched off, including at the hospital and on city streets. Driving was forbidden for everyone except first responders. The blackout also provided the CDC with an opportunity to simulate bombing attacks. The effort would test crisis communication and appraise fire and ambulance response times in total darkness. The blackout was originally scheduled for late December, but the U.S. Army put a moratorium on tests until after the holidays.

The CDC rescheduled it for the evening of Sunday, January 3, 1943. Information about the blackout was provided to the public via radio and through local newspapers, the *Muncie Morning Star* and *Muncie Evening Press*.

The *Star* warned readers the week before that "at the sound of the air-raid alarm, all pedestrians shall take cover until the all clear signal is sounded."[274]

At 10:00 p.m. on January 3, the city's factories blew their whistles, darkly heralding the test. All of Muncie fell pitch black and silent. At 10:10 p.m., the CDC control center dispatched fire and ambulance due to "incendiary bombs at Manhattan avenue and Twelfth street, six casualties." Another crew was dispatched three minutes later at "Hoyt avenue and Twelfth street, high explosive bombs, two casualties." First responders were rushed at 10:19 p.m. to "Neely avenue and Linden street, incendiary bombs, four casualties." At 10:22 p.m., they rushed to "Adams and Walnut streets, high explosive and incendiary bombs, ten casualties."[275]

Bly's photo in Earlham's 1930 *Sargasso* yearbook. *Courtesy of the Internet Archive.*

In the middle of the test, as the din of sirens echoed across the city, the Civilian Defense Control center received a call from a downtown air-raid warden who had a very real emergency. Howard Sheller had been patrolling his district when he tripped over the legs of a dead woman on the sidewalk in front of Hotel Roberts. She had apparently fallen out of an open window. Sheller "routed an emergency call through the civilian defense control center and an ambulance was dispatched to the scene."[276]

The body was identified as Florence Bly, a beloved thirty-five-year-old librarian who had grown up in Muncie. Sheller found Bly dressed in a heavy winter coat with a cloth over her head. "Death apparently was instantaneous," the *Star* reported. "Miss Bly suffered a skull fracture, neck fracture and other injuries."[277]

Police arrived after the air-raid test was over. MPD captain Harry Butler entered Bly's sixth-floor room and found it locked from the inside. The only thing amiss was the open window. The lights were out, apparently in compliance with the air-raid test. The cops only found "a small traveling bag containing personal effects." A note inside peculiarly read, "In case of sudden death, notify the M.L. Meeks Mortuary."[278]

It was unclear if Bly jumped or fell out of the window, but Delaware County coroner John Thornburg ruled out murder. The librarian had registered at the hotel on January 1 "after telling relatives she wished to be alone."[279] Detectives learned that this was a common occurrence, as "she often came to the hotel for brief periods of a few days."[280]

Coroner Thornburg suspected suicide after learning that Bly was "despondent concerning ill health, the war and other causes."[281] She had also been granted a six-week leave of absence from the Muncie Public Library in mid-December. Bly was the head librarian of the Grace Keiser Maring Library in Heekin Park.[282]

On Wednesday, January 5, 1943, the heartbroken staff at Maring closed the branch to attend Bly's funeral at Meeks Mortuary.[283] She was buried with family at Earlham Cemetery in Richmond. Bly's estate in 1943 was valued at $11,000, which is about $200,000 in 2024. In her will, she left money to friends, family and the library.

By the end of the century, Bly's ghost or an apparition looking like Bly was haunting Hotel Roberts. In Frederick Graham's 1997 short history of the hotel, a booklet titled *Radisson Hotel Roberts: Muncie's Historic Treasure*, he wrote about a specter lurking about the upper floors. "This 'guest' is seen occasionally on dark, moonless nights when the streets near the hotel are unusually quiet."[284] On such nights, Munsonians and visitors "see what appears to be a woman peering out one of the windows."[285] The ghost materialized as a "young woman, dressed in neat, dark schoolmarm type clothes."

Graham asked readers, "Could this apparition be the spirit of the Muncie librarian who plunged to her death from her room?" He then recounted the tale of her demise, concluding that her death was an accident after leaning too far out the window to watch the blackout test.

The ghost story was made popular by Tom Baker and Jonathan Tichenal in their 2008 book, *Haunted Indianapolis and Other Indiana Ghost Stories*. The authors wrote that Bly's shade appears "in the guise of a matronly woman in black clothing, wandering through the hallways or standing in the lobby of the Hotel Roberts, waiting for the clerk to appear and check her in for the very last time."[286]

In life, Florence Bly was no stranger to Hotel Roberts. She frequently stayed there as an adult and attended parties in the ballroom during her youth. Her name appeared often in local newspapers in the early twentieth century, allowing me to construct a brief biography. It's clear from these articles that Bly was wicked smart, a talented musician and actress and a beloved librarian. Thousands of children had the pleasure of listening to Bly read to them at the Grace Keiser Maring branch of the Muncie Public Library.

Hotel Roberts in the early 1920s. *Courtesy of Ball State University Libraries' Bracken Archive and Special Collections.*

Florence was born in Richmond, Indiana, on Christmas Eve 1907. After her mother died four years later, she was sent with her sister Eleanor to live in Muncie with their aunt, Elizabeth Mae Puckett. Puckett was the housekeeper of Amos Whiteley, an aged and widowed industrialist. Whiteley had moved to Muncie in 1894 to establish the Whiteley Malleable Castings Company just west of what is now McCulloch Park. His brother William had opened a reaper factory the year before. The brothers made a fortune in local real estate during the gas boom, a legacy that remains today with the Whitely and McKinley neighborhoods. Throughout the 1910s, Amos lived at 906 East Adams with Puckett, the Bly sisters and their cousin Mildred Lamb.

Florence's name appeared every year in local newspapers from 1916 until her death in early 1943. In the first instance, she was identified as a victim in a terrible car accident on Jackson Street in March 1916. Florence was sitting in the backseat of a touring car with her friend Marie Lambert. Bly's older cousin Mildred was driving when a truck slammed into them. Bly and Lambert were "bruised and shaken up." Mildred suffered a "severe nervous shock" and bad "contusions about her head and face."[287]

Florence recovered and attended Washington School for elementary education. While there, she won first prize for best Victory Garden in

Bly was a member of Science Club her Junior Year. She's in the second row from the bottom, fourth person from the left. From *The Magician*, 1925. *Courtesy of Biblioboard Open Access.*

Washington School in the early twentieth century. *Courtesy of the Delaware County Historical Society, Mike Mavis Collection.*

Muncie Central's Senior Orchestra, 1926. Bly is in the front row. From *The Magician*, 1926. *Courtesy of Biblioboard Open Access.*

1918.[288] She attended St. John's Universalist Church and sang in the choir. Bly once performed "The Snowdrops" with Rosemary Ball, Paul Brown and Fred Baldwin at a Sunday service.[289] Around this time, she began playing the violin and gave recitals at church.

Bly honed her talent over the years. She played for Muncie Central's orchestra during high school and gave performances with the Muncie Conservatory of Music. On May 5, 1923, she performed in a Junior Matinee Musical violin concert at the Roberts—Muncie's swank new hotel in downtown Muncie.

Bly flourished at Central. She often made the honor roll, even receiving four As in the fall of 1924. That same year, fellow Juniors voted Bly as best musician. She joined Central's Science, Minuet, Glee and Dramatic Clubs. During her senior year, she was elected to serve as secretary of the student council. Bly also pledged and was admitted to the Sewing Club with Ruth Penzel, Harriet Boyce, Rosemary and Adelia Ball and Jane Oesterle.

The Sewing Club ostensibly was a young women's social club organized around needlework, but it was really a popular high school sorority. At the end of the school year, Bly attended a Sewing Club dance in the Hotel Roberts ballroom. The *Evening Press* reported that she attended wearing "a flame satin crepe with a long scarf hanging from the shoulders to the waist line and caught with a rhinestone buckle."[290]

In the spring of 1925, she was cast as Bella in *Rollo's Wild Oats*, a play performed in Central's auditorium. The *Press* described the performance as funny and well attended. The romance "of Bella the housemaid, played by Florence Bly, and Dave, a hired hand played by Roger Gullett, was an amusing part of the show."[291] She starred her senior year in the Dramatic Club's performance of *The Finger of God*.

Bly's Muncie Central high school senior photo. From *The Magician*, 1926. *Courtesy of the Delaware County Historical Society.*

Bly that year was also elected secretary-treasurer of the Sewing Club. She helped plan several club dinners and dances at the Hotel Roberts. She graduated in spring of 1926, playing the violin with Central's Senior Quartet at the diploma ceremony. Later that night, she attended a party at the Roberts.

Florence was relatively wealthy by the time she graduated. When Amos Whiteley died in 1925, he left his house and furniture to Elizabeth Puckett, Florence's aunt. To cousin Mildred, whom Whiteley referred to in his will as the "real housekeeper," he left $1,000. To Florence, "the high school and musical student of the Whiteley home, a like sum is given."[292]

After Muncie Central, Bly attended Earlham College in Richmond, Indiana. Throughout her college years, Muncie's newspapers mention her frequent visits home. At Thanksgiving in the fall of 1925, for instance, Bly attended a Delta Theta Tau sorority dance at the Hotel Roberts. Later that year, she attended the Sewing Club's New Year's Eve bash, also held at the Roberts. The *Star* noted that Bly went without a date.

In November 1927, she directed a play called *The Youngest* for Central's Dramatic Club while home on break. The club earned $100 in ticket sales. A few weeks later, she attended the Violet Club's New Year's Eve dance at the Hotel Roberts, this time with a beau—Mr. Keith Harrison.

When Florence graduated from Earlham in the spring of 1930, the *Star* published a list of her many college accomplishments. Bly was,

> *social chairman of the class and has been a member of the Y.W.C.A. cabinet, the Women's Athletic Association and the Mantle Dramatic Club. She has the leading role in the senior class play,* The Royal Family, *to be presented June 6 and 14, and has been elected to membership in the Earlham chapter of the National Collegiate Players.*[293]

She returned to Muncie and started working at the Muncie Public Library that summer. In August 1930, Bly was hired "to assist in the adult circulation department" at Carnegie Library downtown.[294] Two months later, when the

Top: Hotel Roberts ballroom in 1931. *Courtesy of Ball State University Libraries' Bracken Archive and Special Collections.*

Bottom: Bly was on the *Sargasso* staff her senior year, as an associate. *Courtesy of the Internet Archive.*

The Grace Keiser Maring branch of the Muncie Public Library, mid-twentieth century. *Courtesy of Ball State University Libraries' Bracken Archive and Special Collections.*

Grace Keiser Maring branch opened in Heekin Park, Bly was moved to assist its daily operations. The following spring, she served as the drama coach for students at Central in the production of *The Nut Farm*.

Being a librarian must have been a good fit because she took a temporary leave in June 1931 to attend a summer library science program at the University of Illinois in Urbana.[295] Bly was promoted to "assistant librarian of the children's department" at Maring Branch when she returned.

In the fall, she started a program reading to children on Saturday mornings titled Story Hour. It was enormously popular—seventy-five children even attended the Saturday before Christmas. She read *How the Seasons Came to Be*, *Why There Is a Hare in the Moon* and *Millions of Cats*.

She took the show on the road around Muncie at first but settled the program at Grace Keiser Maring. To promote Book Week in November 1933, Florence broadcast Story Hour live on WLBC radio.

Bly graduated with a second bachelor's degree in 1933, this time in library science from the University of Illinois. One month later, she was promoted to Maring's head librarian. The *Press* noted her "considerable experience in the junior department."[296]

Two years later, Bly took a leave of absence in the spring of 1935 to visit her brother Kirk in Los Angeles. They vacationed together at the Spa Hotel in Aguascalientes, Mexico. The *Press* reported that she "was accompanied by

Mr. and Mrs. J.D. Miller, and daughter Elizabeth, of Winchester, and Kirk L. Bly, of Los Angeles."[297]

One year later, in April 1936, Florence married John Personnette Trees, a recent widow and violin teacher. The ceremony was performed at St. John's at the corner of Madison and Jackson, with Reverend Arthur McDavitt officiating. "Miss Sally Robards and Merrill Hoseler were attendants."[298] Two months later, Bly attended her ten-year Central class reunion at the Hotel Roberts with Trees. Bly helped organize the reunion since she was student council secretary in high school.

The couple lived at 1709½ South Elm Street, but the marriage didn't last. Florence sued for divorce in 1940. After filing for a change of venue, the split was granted by a Blackford County judge in September 1940.[299]

In that year, Maring Branch library turned ten years old. Bly continued as head librarian, offering weekly Story Hours there and occasionally at Southside schools and churches. The program continued to be a great success. In March 1941, the *Star* reported that "Miss Florence Bly, librarian of Maring Branch Library, has reported an increase in the number of children working for reading diplomas this year."[300]

Just before Christmas 1942, Bly received a temporary leave of absence from work for reasons unknown.[301] At the time, she was living with her aunt Elizabeth Puckett at the Whiteley house on East Adams. The house, if you'll recall, was left to Puckett in Amos Whiteley's will. Sometime after Christmas, Florence told her aunt that she needed to be alone for a few days and checked into the Hotel Roberts on New Year's Day. She was found dead on the sidewalk around 10:15 p.m. on January 3 during the blackout test. The coroner never determined how Florence fell out of the window. He wrote on the death certificate that she died from "falling or jumping from 6th floor window of hotel to side walk."[302]

Despite the tragedy, the Hotel Roberts flourished for many decades. It was closed in 2006 after a few rough years of declining business. After a $17 million renovation, the building reopened exclusively in 2014 as apartments for senior Munsonians. I'm not sure if Florence Bly still haunts the sixth floor.

What is clear is the piercing wail of the air-raid sirens every Friday at 11:00 a.m. The warning system expanded during the Cold War and today serves mostly to warn Delaware County residents of imminent tornados. But now that I've written this story, every time I hear sirens howling across the city on Fridays, I can't help but think of Florence Bly.

What did she see out in the darkness over Muncie so many years ago?

CHAPTER 10

WRAITHS ON THE MACEDONIA TURNPIKE

I n the early spring of 1936, the *Muncie Evening Press* published a series of short ghost stories set in rural southern and eastern Delaware County. The ghostly tales were shared by John Will Gibson, a lifelong county resident and retired schoolteacher. The *Press* plugged the series as "authentic folk tales about spooks that roamed Delaware County in the old days, frightening our ancestors."[303] Gibson recounted a personal ghost story and three others heard directly "from those who say they encountered these wraiths."[304]

Gibson was born just before the Civil War in 1859 and raised on a farm in the northeast corner of Monroe Township—Section 35 to be exact. In the mid-1800s, this area of Delaware County was a busy intersection of travel, with folks coming into and out of Muncie on the southeast side.

Gibson's family farm was located alongside the Macedonia Turnpike, a gravel road that ran from Muncie to the hamlet of Macedonia in southeast Monroe Township. The pike was halfway between the well-traveled Walnut Street Turnpike to the west and the Muncie and New Burlington Turnpike east. An old 1820 federal government road ran along the White River to the northeast, built to connect early Muncietown to Windsor and Winchester in Randolph County. The state's 1832 corduroy Richmond Road also ran through the area, roughly parallel to the pikes.

Gibson grew up near Monroe Township School No. 1 and a log cabin church, located "in the center of a forest of great oak, hickory, black walnut and a few other species of trees." In addition to acres of wetlands, the section of county was "mostly primeval forest, with log houses scattered here and there, and now and then a log church and schoolhouse."[305]

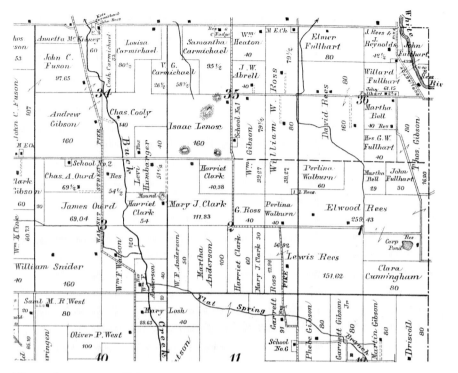

The northeast corner of Monroe Township, a hotbed of paranormal activity in the nineteenth century. Image taken from the 1887 *Atlas of Delaware County*. *Courtesy of the Delaware County Historical Society.*

For most of the nineteenth century, Native American earthworks dating back thousands of years rose above the farm and pastureland in northeast Monroe Township. Although agriculture would eventually destroy them, the mounds remained visible in the mid-1800s as Gibson came of age.

Several family members owned and operated farms in the vicinity. John Gibson's maternal grandfather Stephen Harter had lived in the area and raised eighteen children, including Gibson's mother, Eliza Jane.

Growing up, Gibson was surrounded by his other grandparents, seven siblings and dozens of aunts, uncles and cousins. Gibson wrote that the "community was made up of hard-working men and women who loved home and had large families."[306] Most were "sincerely religious, yet they were full of superstition concerning curious happenings that could not be explained."[307]

WRAITHS ON THE TURNPIKE

John Will Gibson's first ghostly tale came from his father, George, and uncle Nepthalim "Neps" Ross. A few years before John was born, his eighteen-year-old father, George, began courting Eliza Jane Harter, John's soon-to-be-mother. After a date one fine spring evening in 1853, George made his way home, riding his gentle mare Dolly toward the Macedonia Turnpike. The sun had set by the time George and Dolly made it onto the road.

As shadows grew, Dolly's slow, plodding pace soon lulled George to sleep. Then, suddenly, near the Heaton Farm, Dolly "stopped and snorted," snapping George "wide awake."[308]

He looked around in the fading light to see what caused his horse such fret. "To the east of the road was an open field, enclosed by a rail fence. On the west was a large oak tree at the side of the road, with a dense, swampy forest beyond."[309]

Just then, George saw "a snow-white object, very distinct in the mist." He watched as it passed "through the rail fence, as if no obstruction were there." It stopped and remained motionless in the middle of the turnpike.

The specter suddenly lurched forward, freaking out Dolly again, who turned to run. George held the reins fast. He attempted to turn his mare

Hermann Hendrich's 1823 painting, *Will-o'-the-Wisp. Courtesy of Wikimedia Commons.*

back toward the direction of the ghost but couldn't "compel her to go near the uncanny object." George later described it "as having the shape and size of a man with hands on his hips, head missing and robed in a white sheet, slowly moving across the road, stopping at intervals."[310]

Getting nowhere fast, George dismounted and tried to walk Dolly toward the wraith, but the horse wouldn't budge. "The ghostly figure moved slowly...like a shadow might have done and drifted among the trees of the forest, finally to disappear." George mounted his horse and rode fast for home.

At the time, Gibson was living on a farm owned by his sister and brother-in-law Nancy and Neps Ross. The morning after the supernatural encounter, George was eating breakfast with Neps and a farmhand named Jake Lessinger. Neps noticed something amiss and inquired as to what was the matter.

NEPS ROSS.
He Is Said to Be Delaware County's Most Famous Trader.

Neps Ross from the *Muncie Morning Star*, February 19, 1900. *Scanned from microfilm at Ball State University's Bracken Library.*

"Well, I saw something as I came home last night that I cannot explain," George replied. To his astonishment, Neps laughed and said that he, too, had seen the wraith on the turnpike. Neps recounted:

One night when I was walking home from Munsey with my head down, I happened to stub my toe or I might have run into it. When I looked up, I was within two feet of the man or ghost with his head off. I will admit I did not feel very comfortable just then, yet I could not feel it meant any harm to me, although unexplainable things are unpleasant.[311]

Lessinger interjected to remind George and Neps about a decapitated corpse once found in the area: "Don't you remember the tale of the tin peddler?" Sometime back, the headless body of a traveling tin salesman "was found dead under that same tree....I'll bet that's his spirit." Lessinger boasted that "if I ever see that ghost, I'll sure ask it what it wants."[312] He would soon get his chance.

A few weeks later, Lessinger was riding up the Macedonia Turnpike into Muncie when he was "rudely awakened by his mount's snorting, rearing and

I saw the strangest figure.

A ghost appearing in the 1894 book *Phantastes: A Faerie Romance*. *Courtesy of the British Library.*

whirling around on her hind feet." The horse felt something strange and tried to run. Lessinger pulled the reins to a stop just as a wraith floated onto the pike. Whatever it was, it moved in total silence.

Wide eyed and terrified, the horse turned and bolted in the opposite direction, but Lessinger pulled the reins hard. His mount stopped in a

A haunting in a swamp, from the 1893 book *Absolutely True*. *Courtesy of the British Library*.

huff. Together, they turned to face "the white object in the middle of the road." Both horse and man stared down the uncanny apparition, which stared unflinchingly straight back. After a moment of bewilderment, Lessinger whipped his horse around and "spurred her into a dead run for Munseytown."[313]

Lessinger later made it home without incident. He slept in the next day, as George and Neps noticed the tired and strained horse in the barn. Neps asked Jake that afternoon, "What made you abuse your horse in that manner? Did you see the ghost last night?"

Lessinger muttered, "I guess I might as well confess, I did."

George asked if he got a chance to inquire about what the ghost wanted. Lessinger hung his head, saying, "I sure did not, and admit I was never so scared in my life."

MARKSMAN'S BEST FRIEND

There wasn't much by way of passable roads in rural Delaware County prior to the Civil War. Farmers and fieldworkers made their way via rivers, packed dirt and corduroy roads or on narrow footpaths that "led more directly to any place you wished to reach."[314]

The footpaths snaking between rural properties helped farmers quickly get to neighbors. Labor was in short supply in the 1830s and 1840s, so the community relied on cooperation. Neighbors worked often together during harvest season in "log-rolling a house and barn raising, hog-killing and so forth."[315]

Harvest work was arduous and took all day. Picking, reaping and butchering were followed by processing, packing and, when harvests were good, feasting. After, say, a day of slaughtering hogs, the farmers would set about "lard rendering, sausage making, etc., then late supper, pumpkin pie, a sample of the sausage and other pork tidbits, washed down with sweet apple cider, which was sometimes 'hard' as they called it when fermented."[316]

John Gibson's grandfather Stephen Harter was in high demand during the harvest seasons of the 1830s and '40s. Gibson wrote that Grandpa Harter was called on often, "as he had a fine deer rifle and was an excellent marksman."[317]

One harvest, after a busy day of slaughtering pigs, Harter returned home on foot under a "moonless, somewhat misty, hazy, autumn night."[318] He turned down one of the footpaths, bordered on either side "by thickets of hazel and wild roses."[319] A few yards in, he heard the crunching of dead leaves behind him, like something was following.

The marksman "walked slowly on the alert until he came to a small opening often found in primeval forests…Oak Openings." He ran into the center and turned sharply to see what stalked him. There it was, "a great white dog sitting on his haunches, in the middle of the path, about 10 feet away." The spectral beast, or whatever it was, burned "uncommonly white and shone out in the opening."[320]

Harter called out to it, "but the dog did not move." It just sat there, staring calmly at him without making a sound. The farmer ran out of the clearing, and the ghost began to follow, keeping a steady pace and distance.

Harter tried a different tactic. He turned to move "toward the uncanny spectre of a dog." But as soon as he was within ten feet, the spirit vanished. Satisfied but no less creeped out, Harter spun around and ran away. He made it no more than ten paces when the ghostly hound reappeared and began trotting behind.

Gibson wrote that his grandfather was a nervous fellow and decided to end the nonsense the only way he knew how—violence. He drew his rifle and "took careful aim, feeling sure of putting a bullet into the dog's brain." He was an excellent marksman, after all—a butcher of pigs. *Crack.* The air filled with gunpowder smoke, yet the apparition remained. The dog sat unperturbed "on his haunches just about 10 feet away, unharmed."[321] Harter fired twice more, but the creature sat motionless, "calmly resting on his hips."

A terrified Harter ran for home, weaving between footpaths out onto a wider dirt road. The giant ghost dog lumbered behind. When the marksman reached his farm's ancient oak front gate, he turned and steadied his rifle against the railing and fired another shot. The bullet whizzed through the ghost without harm.

Harter bolted to his farmhouse, "keeping his eye on the weird creature, hoping it could not get through the gate or the high rail fence."[322] But it did. The ghost passed right through the closed gate of heavy oak timbers.

By the time Harter reached his house, his wife, Sarah, was on the porch, "Stephen, what in the world are you shooting at?"

Harter motioned for his wife to look toward the small gate at the yard's edge. He whisper-yelled, "Do you see the large white dog just outside?"

"Yes," replied a confused Sarah in a normal speaking voice. "He is a very fine-looking dog."

"He's been following me and acting so queerly I tried to shoot him and could not."

Harter joined his wife on the porch. The couple watched "the strange, white dog pass through the little yard gate as if it was not there." Sarah grabbed her husband's rifle and shot at it. Alas, her bullets passed right through too, as if the ghost was made of mist.[323]

As the apparition started up the steps, the Harters ran into their house. The dog dropped its ghostly white paw in the doorway as Stephen slammed the door shut. He expected "to see the spook dog on the inside as he slowly backed away but he was seen no more."

The next day, Stephen and Sarah looked for paw prints along the muddy path and found nothing. Stephen inquired at neighboring farms about strange dog-like creatures roaming the forest, but no one had any clue what he was talking about. The ghostly hound was never seen again.

THE GRAVEYARD WRAITHS

Rees Cemetery lies not far from Gibson's family farm in the northwest corner of Perry Township. The West Fork of the White River flows a short distance just north. Burlington Drive, once known as the Muncie and New Burlington Turnpike, runs parallel to the river immediately south of the cemetery.

The graveyard was named in honor of the Rees family, who settled the area. By the end of the nineteenth century, Reeses owned large estates across Perry and Monroe Townships.

One of these farms was owned and managed by Morris Rees, son of family progenitor Judge Lewis Rees. Morris's farm sprawled along Burlington Pike about a mile north of New Burlington. John Gibson wrote that an orphaned boy lived nearby and was friends with John Rees, Morris's son, from whom Gibson first heard the story.

One night, this unnamed friend of John Rees was walking home, whistling and singing "to drive away any fears that might beset him on that misty, foggy night of early spring."[324]

He rounded the gentle corner and saw Rees Cemetery looming on the hill in front of him. At the time of the story, the graveyard sat among a grove of "great trees of oak, sycamore and willow."[325] Even in daylight, their heavy shadows stretched out over the road. A small brook runs to this day

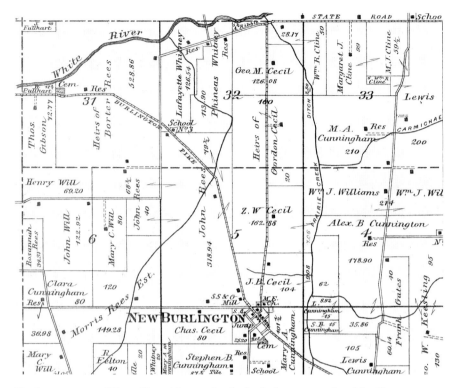

Northwest corner of Perry Township, another hotbed of paranormal activity. Rees Cemetery is at top left. Image taken from the 1887 *Atlas of Delaware County. Courtesy of the Delaware County Historical Society.*

through the area, attracting vocal frogs and strange birds making noise in the darkness.

After John's friend crossed the bridge, he heard "a deep moaning screech that seemed to come from the tombstones of the departed." And there "to his horror, stood a tall object in a snow-white robe."

Just as the boy "caught a glimpse of this frightful apparition, it began to move toward the road." As it did, the wraith threw its head back and sent forth an "unearthly moan ending in a scream that made his knees knock together."[326]

"This uncanny object was out of the ordinary, so vaguely mysterious, so unearthly, that it could not be reasonably explained."[327] The "spirit-like figure passed through the old rail fence just as a shadow would have done."

The ghost reached the road and stood bolt upright. It turned and stared down the boy. After a moment, the wraith opened its mouth impossibly wide and unleashed another hideous "blood-curdling moan, ending again in a hair-raising screech." It then turned at an uncanny speed, "flitted through the brush hedge south of the road" and disappeared.[328]

The boy ran all the way home. Gibson said his night was filled "by fitful sleep and horrible dreams of spectres and ghosts."

THE JACK-O-LANTERN OF SIMONTON FARM

The final ghostly encounter was experienced by John Will Gibson himself while riding with his brother Charlie one evening in the 1850s. The brothers were coming home from Eaton when they found themselves trotting along John Simonton's farm in southeast Union Township, about a mile east of Shideler along Rocky Branch Creek. The Gibson brothers rode together on the same horse.

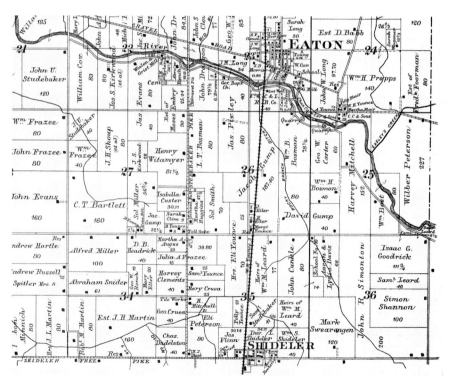

John Simonton's farm was in the southeast corner of Union Township. Image taken from the 1887 *Atlas of Delaware County. Courtesy of the Delaware County Historical Society.*

Ignis fatuus, bog light or irricht. Joseph Gabriel Frey, 1878. *Courtesy of the Wellcome Library.*

Their pace was slow when Charlie spotted something strange moving fast across Simonton's farm. "What do you suppose John is chasing after with his lantern? Do you see him? I didn't think he could run that fast?"

John Gibson turned to see what his brother was going on about. "That is not Mr. Simonton. He could not run that fast; neither could you nor I." John didn't think it was a ghost but rather "something I have always prayed to see, for that's a jack-o'-lantern."

Today, we use the term "jack-o-lantern" to describe carved pumpkins, a typical Halloween decoration found across the United States and beyond. However, for many years, jack-o-lantern meant will-o'-the-wisp—a supposed atmospheric phenomenon of glowing methane gas floating at night over swamps, bogs and wetlands.

Such ghost lights were also known variously as friar's lantern, ghost candles, bog lights, irrlicht, wandering light, *ignis fatuus* (fools fire), hobby lantern, hinkypunk and spooklights. John Gibson described it: "The swampy, marshy land of the day under certain conditions of the surrounding atmosphere, especially during the spring thaws, would exude a warm, gaseous vapor in the form of a white cloud."

Charlie didn't seem to care and slapped the horse's reins. "Here's where I speed off for home," he yelled back at his brother. "I never prayed to see a thing like that and if you wish to see it, jump off."

John calmed his anxious sibling and compelled "him to watch this rare sight." The spooky bog light was following a "little open drain, twisting and turning as it does to find its way to the big ditch yonder, riding on the east wind."

Alas, this *ignis fatuus* "ghost reached the big open ditch and followed it to the grove about 80 rods away, where we could see it flitting among the trees just as if it were a real lantern." The light disappeared, and the brothers made for home.

JAMES MUSCO

John Will Gibson ends the series with a short dialogue, supposedly spoken by James Musco, a Native American man who lived with the Rees family in the mid-1800s. For reasons history does not record, Musco and his parents, Jacob and Sally, stayed or possibly returned to Delaware County after the Lenape left in 1820. James was a teenager at the time. The Muscos initially lived in Munseytown near the river.

After James's parents died, he lived on the Lewis and Mary Rees farm in Perry Township, where he became good friends with Rees's sons Morris and Borter. As an adult, Musco was a talented carpenter and well known across Delaware County.

There are *many* stories about Musco; most of them aren't true or include details without a way to verify. Musco left no writings nor gave any interviews about his life. He died on November 17, 1873, and was buried at Rees Cemetery.

Gibson attempts to debunk some of the hauntings with a rational explanation given by Musco to one of the Rees boys. He writes Musco's dialogue in a racist way, using broken English in a manner representing a stereotypical mid-twentieth-century Hollywood character. I won't repeat it here, but Gibson's Musco basically says that the tree limbs above Rees Cemetery rubbed together in such a way to cause a terrible screeching, not dissimilar to what John Rees's orphan friend once heard when he passed by the cemetery. It wasn't a ghost after all, just wind. "The trees groaned and the ghost moved at the same time…the excited condition of the mind did the rest."[329]

CHAPTER 11

THREE COUNTY TALES OF THE UNCANNY

Delaware County is full of cemeteries. They scatter across the landscape in all twelve townships—a foremost commonality among all. Not every death ends in a burial, nor do all burials occur in cemeteries, but the ground on which we live is filled with tombs of our forebears.

The Indiana Department of Natural Resources' State Historic Architectural Research Database and Structures Map, which is thankfully abbreviated to SHAARD, surveys seventy-five cemeteries in Delaware County.[330] These burial grounds range in size from tiny Hoover Cemetery in New Burlington, with about a dozen burials, to massive cemeteries like Beech Grove in Muncie, with more than forty-five thousand.[331]

However, a few dozen graveyards don't make this list. Goldsmith Gilbert's cemetery mentioned in the third chapter, the story of the seven-year icehouse ghost, is a good example. Those originally entombed were, supposedly, disinterred and reburied at Beech Grove in the 1840s. Gilbert's old boneyard was forgotten as such and later developed for housing and commercial property.

At least two Native American cemeteries existed in Delaware County, although they don't make the list either. After the feds pushed the Lenape out of Indiana, their cemetery in Munseytown was ransacked by white settlers. The Munsee speakers living on the bluff overlooking the bend of the White River buried their dead in a graveyard just west of what is now Walnut Street, on the grounds of Minnetrista Museum and Gardens.[332]

Early 1900s Beech Grove Cemetery postcard. *Courtesy of Ball State University Libraries' Bracken Archive and Special Collections.*

Cemeteries are often thought to be haunted places, a natural assumption given what's buried there. Graveyards are full of our dead, so it's logical to reckon that their spirits lurk about the place. With but few exceptions, the stories in this book demonstrate that Muncie and Delaware County's ghosts historically were everywhere *but* the cemetery. It's pop culture that tells us otherwise.

The late John Carlson, a reporter for the *Muncie Evening Press* and, later, the *Star Press*, posed the question in 2008 to Tom Schnuck, then superintendent of Beech Grove Cemetery: "Are there even shadowy tales of hauntings associated with the municipal burial ground?"[333]

"Not really," Schnuck replied. Carlson made a point to note that Schnuck took "just a moment's hesitation" before answering. But then, Beech Grove's super recalled that some years prior, a cemetery worker claimed to see a phantom woman floating about the tombstones. "He'd swear up and down that he saw that woman walking around the cemetery."[334]

I heard at least a dozen "haunted cemetery" stories growing up in Delaware County. Specifics were always lacking, and each account turned out to be some dumb generic midwestern folktale. There's just not much evidence in the historical record of ghosts haunting local cemeteries. When spirits did return, they haunted places frequented by the living.

WILLIAM VINCENT RETURNS

William Vincent's ghost was an exemplar. When William Hearn Vincent died in August 1878, he was buried at Bethel Church Cemetery but haunted the house next door. At the time of his death, the cemetery was located on Vincent's farm, along with Bethel Methodist Church and Niles Township Schoolhouse No. 2. The township no longer used the school as such in the late 1870s, and it was converted into a home.

In his will, Vincent left the remodeled school and much of the farm to his daughter Margaret and her husband, Francis Shrack. About six months after Vincent died, the Shracks "moved into the schoolhouse about one hundred yards from the church."[335] The property was just north of where the Albany and Eaton Turnpike turned south toward Albany.

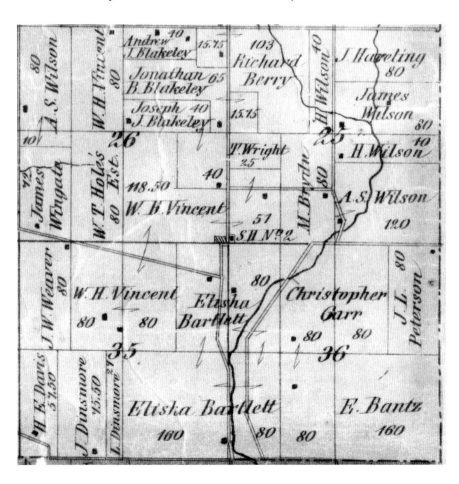

Opposite: William Vincent's farm in Niles Township, 1870s. *Courtesy of Ball State University Libraries' Bracken Archive and Special Collections.*

Above: Bethel Methodist Church on the old William Vincent homestead in 1969. *Courtesy of Ball State University Libraries' Bracken Archive and Special Collections.*

Left: Early twentieth-century artist rendering of a ghost visiting a farmer. John McCutcheon. *Courtesy of the Library of Congress.*

On September 30, 1879, the *Muncie Morning News* reported on the front page that the Shracks "have been annoyed by a peculiar noise emanating from various parts of their home." It had gone on for a while, but they kept mum about it, fearing ridicule. The noises, however, had become "so monotonous that they concluded to expose it."[336]

The Shracks said that "at different times the ghost of Mr. Vincent is seen in the yard, walking around, and that it appears and disappears." Once while eating breakfast, "a tremendous jar of the house was felt." A thorough search revealed "no evidence of anything that would tend to 'shake' the house."

Vincent's ghost also had the habit of knocking on the front door at inconvenient hours. Each time Margaret or Francis answered, "Nobody is to be seen." The most terrifying haunting occurred when Vincent's ghost rained down an uncanny racket on the roof one night. It "sounded like the dropping of silver dollars."[337]

The Shracks took it all in stride. The *News* wrote that "they are not frightened to any great extent over the strange noise and the numerous appearances of Mr. Vincent's ghost."[338]

GRIM SPECTERS AT SHARON MILL

A few miles south of Vincent's farm lay the hamlet of Clifton. The settlement sat on the south bank of Mississinewa River in Section 16 of Delaware Township. Clifton grew to become a small river port and agricultural processing center before the Civil War.

Most of Clifton's commercial activity centered on mills. The first was a crude endeavor built around 1830 by a squatter named John Boyles. Granville Hastings built another mill and race a few years later. Then in 1864, Benjamin Zehner constructed a three-story mill on the river. It remained in operation for decades. Sometime in the 1840s, the county built a dirt road connecting Muncietown to Granville by way of Clifton.

A post office also existed in Clifton from 1853 to 1884, although it was named Sharon. The U.S. Post Office didn't allow two offices with identical or similar names to operate in the same state. A Clifton post office already existed in Union County, Indiana, so the folks living on the Mississinewa named theirs "Sharon" in honor of a local family with that surname. After it opened in 1853, most folks in Delaware County referred to Clifton as Sharon or Sharon Mill.

Zehner Mill in Clifton/Sharon, circa 1890. *Courtesy of Ball State University Libraries' Bracken Archive and Special Collections.*

John Leech's "A Ride Home," 1841. *Courtesy of Old Book Illustrations.*

So, too, did visitors like William Jenkins of Union City. In early January 1893, Jenkins was traveling through Delaware County selling the biography of Jay Gould, a prominent American railroad industrialist and robber baron. It was winter at the time, and snow blanketed the ground. Jenkins traveled in a horse-drawn sleigh.

After a day of selling books around Sharon, Jenkins ate dinner at one of his customer's houses and set off down the old dirt road toward Muncie. When the book salesman was about two miles southwest of the hamlet, he came across "an old moss-covered log stable, constructed many years ago."[339]

As Jenkins passed the old horse barn in the cold, snowy night, he felt a deep sense of unease. "The first intimation I had of anything being wrong was when my horse began to snort with fear."[340] The animal began to rear and threatened to overturn the sleigh. The air then pierced with "a terrible, blood-curdling scream" emanating from the stable.

The horse at that point lost its damn mind and bolted, pulling Jenkins fast down the road in his sleigh. The book peddler turned and "was horrified to see a ghastly looking woman dressed in white with blood pouring from an awful wound in her throat." The phantom "appeared to be skimming over the ground" and was followed by another shade, "that of a man who carried a large corn knife."[341]

Jenkins's horse ran "as fast as possible" toward Muncie as the apparitions faded away into the snowy distance. When he arrived, Jenkins told everyone about the encounter, including reporters at the *Herald*.

They wrote that in old Clifton, "settlers place some credence to Jenkins' story." Fifty years prior in the 1840s, a couple with the surname Josephs lived in a log cabin near the stable. Mr. Josephs "was a shiftless sort of fellow, and one night quarreled with his wife over some trivial matter. Mrs. Josephs ran from the house and took refuge in the old barn, where she was found by her husband who cut her throat with a large butcher knife."[342]

"The affair is very peculiar," a *Herald* reporter told Munsonians, but "Jenkins swears he saw the ghosts."[343]

THE GHOST OF SINA LENOX

In the southern part of Delaware County lies the unincorporated village of Cowan. The community was originally platted in 1869 as McCowan Station, a rural depot along the Fort Wayne, Muncie and Cincinnati Railroad (today

McCOWAN CHAPEL.

Left: McCowan Chapel in Cowan, Monroe Township. Engraving is from Thomas Helm's *History of Delaware County* (1881). *Courtesy of the Delaware County Historical Society.*

Below: Double-exposure "spirit" photo from 1910. G.S. Smallwood. *Courtesy of the Library of Congress.*

Opposite: "The Ghost," circa 1874. Melander and Brother. *Courtesy of the Library of Congress.*

Norfolk Southern). Cowan was named after Charles McCowan, a wealthy settler who donated money for the establishment of a church and school in the village. A post office opened in 1870 but was named by its first postmaster as just "Cowan." The village soon followed suit.

By century's end, Cowan had become a bustling agricultural processing and shipping center (via railroad), with sawmills, a carpentry shop, blacksmith, tile factory and two dry goods stores.

The village grew to become the largest urban center in Monroe Township. In the late nineteenth century, Cowan attracted the sons and daughters of many township settlers, including John P. Lenox and Sina Skinner. The two were married on April 4, 1888. The *Muncie Daily Times* reported that the couple wedded "last evening by and at the residence of W.W. Ross in Monroe township."[344]

Sina suffered mental illness for much of their marriage. She attempted suicide in July 1894 by cutting her throat. "The gash was a dangerous one," the *Times* told readers, "but not necessarily fatal." She was treated by a local doctor, who initially expected her to recover.[345] Alas, the wound proved fatal, and Sina died three days later. She was only twenty-seven.

Just before she died, Sina "summoned the members of her family and other friends to her bedside and bade them an affectionate farewell and asked them to meet her in heaven."[346] Her family buried her at Rees Cemetery, and "a large concourse of friends were in attendance" at the funeral.[347]

One year later, her ghost returned to haunt John Lenox. On July 17, 1895, the *Muncie Morning News* wrote that while "haunted houses in Delaware county are a scarcity…the residents of Cowan, a village six miles south of

STEREOSCOPIC GROUPS & PORTRAITS

Melander, PHOTOGRAPHER, 88 N. Clark St. CHICAGO.

Entered according to Act of Congress by L. M. MELANDER & BRO., in the office of the Librarian of Congress at Washington.

7.—The Ghost.

Muncie, say that they have a haunted house."[348] Apparently, ever since Sina died, "the woman's ghost has paced the streets and alleys of Cowan."

Sometime later, the Lenox house was rented out to another family, "who have become quite well acquainted with this ghost." At night, "screeches and low moans can be heard about the premises and often a female appears at one of the windows." The apparition was "ghastly white and attired in white garments." It wouldn't stay long, giving "a few pitiful wails and bids farewell."[349]

The house was eventually sold to an old man who kept it as a rental. By the summer of 1895, he couldn't keep any tenants due to the hauntings. The new owner didn't believe in ghosts and suspected that neighbors were attempting to drive down the price of the property by "making him believe the house is haunted" so he'd "sell the property at a nominal price."

He let it be known that should the hauntings continue, "the *News* will be permitted to print an item about a real live ghost being filled with buckshot or pierced by a bullet."[350]

CHAPTER 12

ALL HALLOWS' EVE
IN THE MAGIC CITY

The word *holiday* derives from the Old English word *hāligdæg*, which means "holy day." Every culture has them—sacrosanct days set apart from the rest. On such days we're obliged to *observe* something, often with ritualized thought or action. These special days also help us *remember* collectively in a religious or secular way, sometimes both. In the very least, sacred days provide reprieve from the enduring monotony of modern life and, with any luck, a little time off work.

You can tell much about a culture by observing how they ceremonialize their special days. For instance, on New Year's, I often step outside just after midnight to listen to the cacophony of gunfire and fireworks erupting across west Muncie. I find myself asking, "Does every city celebrate the new year with so much gunpowder?" I suppose the answer depends on the character of the residents.

Holidays, especially old ones, also offer a study in cultural change over time—glimpses into our forebear's undulating temperament and imagination, their beliefs and values and the world in which they lived. In a more transcendent way, holidays bond us with foremothers and forefathers who celebrated similar observances—a rhythm of culture that beats annually across generations.

My favorite holiday is Halloween, mostly because I just like the vibe. I think it's good to be reminded annually of the dead, our own deaths and the process of dying. Even though the day has evolved into a cartoonish celebration in the United States, Halloween has meaningful traditions rooted in European Christian and pagan history.

In Celtic lands in northwest Europe, November 1 was a time to celebrate the harvest at summer's end. For Gaelic peoples in Ireland, Scotland and the Isle of Man, the twenty-four-hour day following sundown on October 31 was known as Samhain ("*sow*-in"). The special day fell about halfway between the autumnal equinox and winter solstice. Samhain was marked with bonfires, feasting, mumming and guising (wearing costumes and going door to door), divining the future and leaving food out for returning spirits of departed loved ones.

Samhain was also a time when the space between living and dead worlds thinned to a point of permeability. Some Gaelic peoples believed that supernatural creatures named *Aos Sí* could be contacted on the holy eve of Samhain, along with spirits of the dead. Lesley Pratt Bannatine summarized it nicely in her 1990 book *Halloween*:

> *The festival of Samhain was the most sacred of all Celtic festivals. Its rituals helped link people with their ancestors and the past. The Celts believed that the dead rose on the eve of Samhain and that ancestral ghosts and demons were set free to roam the earth. Since the spirits were believed to know the secrets of the afterlife and the future, the priests of the Celts and Druids held that on the eve of Samhain predictions had more power and omens could be read with more clarity.*[351]

In the Early Middle Ages (i.e., the European Dark Ages) the Roman Catholic Church developed All Hallows' Day or Hallowmas (All Saints' Day) as a sacred holiday to honor departed saints. The vigil the night before became known as All Hallows' Eve and, later, just Hallowe'en. All Hallows' was followed by All Souls' on November 2—a day devoted to remembrance and prayer for all faithful dead.

Together, the triduum became known as Allhallowtide. The church originally celebrated the feast in mid-May to coincide with Lemuralia, an old pagan holiday during which ancient Romans ceremonially removed ghosts from their homes. Around 800 CE, the church shrewdly moved Hallowmas to November 1 to coincide with Samhain and related Celtic festivals in northwest Europe.

In the centuries that followed, Samhain and All Hallows' influenced and developed alongside each other and, ultimately, into each other. As millions of Irish, Scottish and Scots-Irish settlers poured into North America, they brought with them traditions from the old country to form something new: American Hallowe'en.

Halloween postcard, early 1900s. *Courtesy of the Wellcome Collection.*

Here in twenty-first-century Muncie, October 31 is ceremonialized mostly in the evening with trick-or-treating, house parties and garish displays of seasonal accoutrements. An occasional "haunted" house or corn maze pops up in October, along with sharp increases of activity in pumpkin markets.

Lots of people, of all ages, dress up and attend parties of varying licentiousness, while others fill their 'Eve with horror movies. Young masked Munsonians, chaperoned by their ever-hovering parents, of course, prowl streets across Delaware County searching for compliant neighbors to dispense mass-produced sugary treats.

In the nineteenth century, however, unchaperoned children roamed the urban landscape as malevolent gremlins bent on mischief. From the mid-1800s to the mid-1900s, Muncie's teenage boys observed Hallowe'en with mayhem, property destruction and devilish pranks.

An old-timer once reminisced in the *Muncie Morning News* that on one Halloween night in the early 1850s, someone he knew decided to play a vile prank on a train engineer. The impish fiend "took some old clothes, stuffed them full of straw and placed the dummy on the track. Soon a train came thundering along and ran over the thing." Naturally distraught, the engineer backed the train up but found "a twenty-five-cent suit of clothes stuffed with straw instead of a mangled corpse."[352]

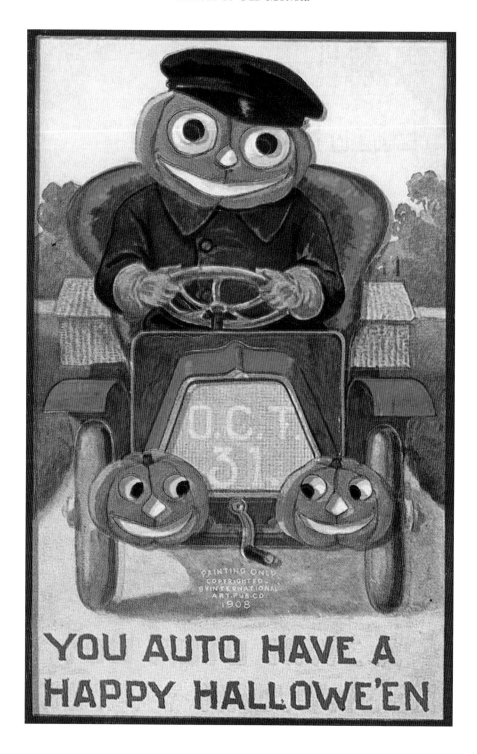

Opposite: Halloween postcard, early 1900s. *Courtesy of the Wellcome Collection.*

Above: Patterson Building, early 1900s. *Courtesy of Ball State University Libraries' Bracken Archive and Special Collections.*

In the 1870s, young hooligans had a tradition every Halloween to place "Dr. Bull's Cough Syrup sign over a meat shop" or "a Milwaukee Lager Beer banner in front of the YMCA."[353] On November 1, 1881, the *Morning News* reported that Halloween pranksters had thrown rotten cabbage against dozens of front doors in downtown, while also throwing "Will Thomas's express wagon on the Jefferson school fence."[354]

In the years after the Civil War, Muncie's residents, especially the affluent ones, held masked parties and fancy balls to celebrate Allhallowtide. In 1882, dozens of Munsonians attended Halloween parties at the homes of the Shick, Gregory, Hart and Heath families.[355]

A masquerade ball was held that year at the Patterson Building. Sponsored by the Muncie Dancing Club, "the attendance was large and a most delightful evening was spent in tripping the light fantastic to the inspiring strains of the German Quadrille Band."[356] About thirty couples attended the party, which didn't end until 4:00 a.m. on All Saints'.

Such festivities continued into the 1890s. Munsonians in that decade also began throwing Halloween street parties downtown with some extravagance. The city, much like the rest of east-central, had begun a radical transformation into an industrial economy after the discovery of natural gas. Rapid economic growth brought many new businesses and dozens of factories. Delaware County's new economy brought enormous wealth and a class of young residents with expendable income.

Muncie also became a regional hub for commercial, retail and entertainment activity during the boom. Electric trolley lines laid in the 1890s connected suburban neighborhoods to downtown and Center Township factory sites. The system provided Greater Muncie residents with reliable and fast transportation to work but also easy access to downtown stores, banks, theaters, hotels, wholesalers, livery stables, houses of worship, saloons, groceries, inter-city stream train depots and brothels.

By 1910, an electric railway system known as the Interurban was snaking across central Indiana, linking Muncie with the region's cities, towns and villages. In the boom years, hundreds and sometimes thousands of people used these transit systems to make their way downtown for holiday festivals like the Fourth of July and Halloween.

Muncie's Halloween street celebrations began around 1890 and continued intermittently until the Great Depression in the 1930s. The festivities often centered on masked parades at sundown. In some years, a well-organized street party drew thousands, while in others, only a dozen poorly masked townies showed up downtown. The scope and size of the festivals depended on weather, the day of the week on which All Hallows' fell and the competence of parade organizers.

The *Muncie Morning News* reported on November 1, 1893, that "Hallowe'en in Muncie…is as big as the Fourth of July and just as noisy." The parade began just after 6:30 p.m. when the sun set. "They came in pairs, in trios, in crowds and singly," the *News* wrote. "They wore everything from grandmother's old house dress to a grand ball masque costume. A 'Cinderilla' tripped down Main street, and if she had worn crystal slippers, her feet would have looked like glass canal boats." Santa Claus followed, escorting "a nun whose sober garments contrasted harmoniously with the red habit of mephisto."[357]

Munsonians held a similar parade the next year. On All Saints' Day in 1894, the *News* wrote that "Halloween is to Muncie, on a small scale, what the Mardi Gras is to New Orleans. It is a fete of masking and merry making."[358] Parties were held all over the city. Munsonians "roasted chestnuts, counted apple seeds and peeled apples and found initials in the peelings, they walked downstairs into the cellar backwards and looked into mirrors at midnight."[359]

Halloween postcard, early 1900s. *Courtesy of the Wellcome Collection.*

The Halloween of 1895 began when a 6.7-magnitude earthquake threw Munsonians out of bed at 5:15 a.m. The *News* reported the next day that residents were "badly frightened by the disturbance. The shock was so great that buildings were shaken and windows rattled, and a general commotion was the result."[360]

The earthquake was centered on the New Madrid Fault near Charleston, Missouri. Shaking was felt as far away as Chicago, Boston and Canada. Luckily for Muncie, the *Times* reported only two damaged buildings in the city: shattered plaster in "Clark Gibson's home on south Monroe Street" and a displaced "steeple on the Church of God, located at the corner of Second and Elm streets."[361]

The Halloween omen was apparently ignored, as "five thousand people, who did not always keep on the sidewalks," jammed downtown Muncie for the All Hallows' Eve parade that night.[362] Crowds formed early in the evening to watch revelers "wearing grotesque costumes, together with the blowing of horns and the operation of various noise producing, nerve destroying apparatuses, marked the presence of the annual festival of foolishness and mischief making."[363] The festival stretched from Main Street south to the Big Four Tracks (CSX) and from Madison to Walnut.

Rain ruined the Halloween of 1897, scuttling plans for a downtown celebration. A few diehards in masks lingered on Walnut Street, but eventually everyone went indoors. Ignoring the weather, one hundred couples celebrated the night at a Halloween dance in Shirk's Hall. The highlight of the evening was the costume of one reveler, "her false face was made of a pumpkin, and for a nose was a parsnip, six inches long. With a garb that was befitting this head gear, she danced and did not lose her face."[364]

The street festival returned in 1898. The *Press* remarked on All Saints' that "Hallowe'en was celebrated last evening with all its old time vigor and enthusiasm."[365] Munsonians held house parties all over town. The *News* reported that "merriment reigned supreme in scores of Muncie's homes last night, as has been the custom in the Magic City on Hallowe'en evening for years gone by."[366]

The weather was perfect, although downtown crowds were "not so numerous on the streets as has been the custom in former years." However, the city's retail trade was good. Muncie's merchants "dealing in Hallowe'en furnishings declared that the trade was never so prosperous."[367]

The parade began after sundown as usual and continued until about 9:00 p.m. "when many of those en masque went to Shirk's Hall, where the Evening Star Social club gave a masquerade ball. Others went to several parties and dances in different parts of the city."[368]

Segregated at the time, Muncie's African American community held a masked ball at Franklin Hall, sponsored by B. McKinney Ward and John Davis. The *News* wrote the next day that "the hall was never in a better condition than it was last night, and everyone present enjoyed themselves until the wee small hours."[369] An all-Black band known as the Warfield Orchestra provided the night's music. Those in attendance included "E.B. Martin, who represented a football player; Dora Wallace and Nora Morin, two little girls in pink; Etta Shoecraft and Bertha Holland, two girls in pink; the Morin sisters were the most artistically and beautifully dressed and represented the 'Two Red Birds.'"[370]

Halloween mischief and pranks continued in Muncie through the boom. On Halloween 1899, "Some fences and some minor articles that were not chained down suffered," the *News* reported.[371] Just after midnight on All Saints' Day, a "log wagon that has stood in front of Wachtell and Son's store was seen to move southward as if by magic. It actually climbed the fence in the court-house yard, and in some manner disappeared on the inside of the building."[372]

Big crowds returned to downtown Muncie on All Hallows' Eve 1900. The *Times* wrote that "nowhere is Hallowe'en celebrated as it is in Muncie. Persons who have lived elsewhere and who were in Muncie last evening for their first Hallowe'en, say it was a revelation to them."[373] Thousands of people, locals and regional visitors "crowded the streets uptown to view the masqueraders."[374]

The parade began as the sun sank below the horizon. A *Times* reporter spotted a reveler dressed as the devil "paraded arm-in-arm with a beautiful, white-winged angel. A clown accompanied a minister...and a lion ramped and roared beside a meek little lamb. It was a night of gayety, witchery, hobgoblins and unalloyed merriment."[375]

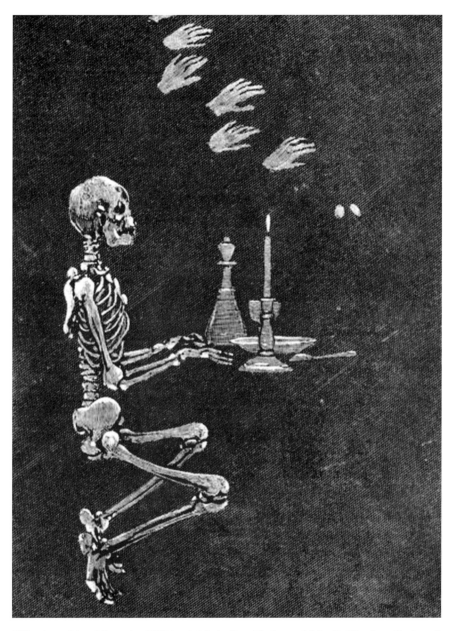

"The Apparition," from the 1897 book *Magic: Stage Illusions and Scientific Diversions. Courtesy of the Wellcome Collection.*

The *Star*'s write-up about Halloween in the next day's paper was more flowery. It perhaps serves better as a description of how Munsonians understood the holiday at the turn of the century:

It was regarded as the time of all others when supernatural influences prevail, and as a night which was set apart for a universal walking abroad of spirits, both of the visible and invisible world; for on this mystic evening it was believed that even the human spirit might detach itself from the body and wander abroad.[376]

The *Star* also provided a thorough description of the masked parade-goers, including costumes that reflected white people's racism and bigotry of the day:

[From the] *fancy to the grotesque—dudes and dukes, noblemen and grandees, Gypsy maidens, Indians and their princesses, clowns and buffoons, rag-muffins and tramps, Negro wenches, topsides, policeman, white caps, old maids, preachers, priests and nuns, school girls and school boys, dunces, shepherds, musicians, Chinamen, soldiers, rough riders, beggars, harlequins, weary-will "booze fighters" (with the tin can adjunct to their make up), and almost every conceivable description of masquerade. Even "Uncle Sam" was not forgotten in the run of comical take-offs.*[377]

Rain ruined the street carnival in 1901, but a massive, costumed skating party was held at Petty's Auditorium on East Adams Street. The venue was built by brothers Walter and Lon Petty in 1901 as a roller-skating hall and large event space. On November 1, the *Evening Press* reported that "at the Petty auditorium, a large crowd was present. Probably 300 persons were on skates, while a great many more filled the seats to await the prize program of the evening."[378]

A masked Halloween celebration was repeated at Petty's the next year; the "crowd was large and much interest was taken in the affair."[379] Nice weather also allowed for a successful street parade and carnival. The *Press* wrote that "Hallowe'en masqueraders thronged the streets of Muncie from 7:30 o'clock till nearly midnight." Thousands paraded in masks, "grotesque costumes, weird costumes and pretty costumes were to be seen everywhere. Walnut and Main street were lined with a surging mass of people."[380]

Boys ransacked the city, "streets and sidewalks were littered with boxes and barrels, fences were torn down, gates were torn from their hinges and carried

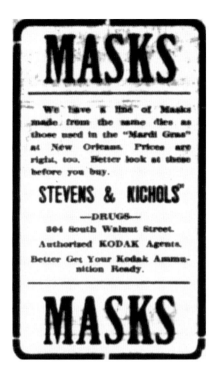

Left: An ad for Halloween masks from Stevens & Nichols on South Walnut. *Scanned from microfilm at Ball State University's Bracken Library.*

Below: Petty's Auditorium near the corner of Jefferson and Adams. *Courtesy of the Delaware County Historical Society, Mike Mavis Collection.*

blocks away, porches were strewn with cabbage and tomatoes and houses were besmeared with paint." In the nearby Normal City suburb, "gates were removed from their hinges and hung on the tops of telephone poles, and boardwalks were propped against doors. Outbuildings were taken off their foundations and faced the wrong way and bicycle racks were placed in inaccessible places."[381]

Muncie's biggest public Halloween celebration of the Indiana Gas and Oil Boom occurred in 1906.[382] Early that October, the *Muncie Star* reported that "merchants, manufacturers, professional men, and trade unionists" had met in the Commercial Club's smoky parlors to hatch a plan for a grand Halloween festival downtown.

To avert criticism of lawlessness and perhaps to remove any stink of paganism, planners innocuously named it the "Fall Fun Festival." The steering committee hoped that it would be a "glorious and

From an ad in the *Muncie Morning Star*, October 30, 1906. *Scanned from microfilm at Ball State University's Bracken Library.*

scintillating pageant surpassing in splendor any exhibition of modern times, one bewildering cyclone of mirth and merriment."[383]

Boosters planned for the festival to include a football game, a hot-air balloon exhibition, barbecue, street vaudeville, fireworks, an electric light display and an outdoor costumed ball on High Street. The steering committee also arranged for three grand parades: the Industrial Parade led by the King of Enterprise; the Floral Parade honoring the Queen of Halloween; and, at sunset, the Parade of the Masqued Courtiers. This last spectacle was to include "hundreds of leaping demons, weird specters, funny clowns and strangely costumed forms of every description."[384]

Charles Fairbanks, the vice president of the United States, was also scheduled to speak in Muncie on Halloween. Fairbanks was stumping for Republican candidates around the Hoosier State in the week before the midterm elections. After his speech was announced, Muncie's Democrats accused the city's Republicans of using the festival as a political rally.

This was true given the outsized role that Muncie's young GOP industrialists played in planning the event. In response, local Republicans disinvited the vice president from speaking in Muncie to "remove all politics from the great day of merrymaking."[385]

Who needs a vice president when you have the King of Enterprise? It's not clear how the king was selected, but His Majesty's identity remained concealed behind a mask until the coronation ceremony. The King of Enterprise represented "the spirit of progressiveness and hustle which has characterized the career of the Magic City."[386]

The Queen of Halloween, however, was chosen by popular vote to be "the ruler of all the gay crowd of maskers, which will throng her court on the evening of Halloween."[387] After a heated race, Munsonians selected Modjeska Silvers with 10,807 votes.

The city buzzed with preparations in the weeks leading up to All Hallows' Eve. The committee eventually secured DePauw and Rose Polytechnic (Rose-Hulman) to play the afternoon football game. The *Muncie Daily Herald* wrote that "considerable 'dope' has been circulating concerning the teams of the rival institutions and every indication points toward a most exciting game."[388]

Union Traction advertised special runs of Halloween Interurban cars between Muncie and neighboring communities, the idea being that *all* east-central Indiana was invited to the festival. The new terminal at the southeast corner of Mulberry and Charles was scheduled to open on Halloween. "Special rates on all steam lines"[389] were also issued for anyone coming into Muncie via train on October 31.

Four days before the event, Mayor Leonidas Guthrie ceremonially resigned "the supervision of the city to the King of Enterprise" and issued a proclamation decreeing the streets cleared for the parades. He also banned the sale of firearms and ordered celebrants to not carry "heavy clubs, canes or sticks for improper purposes." For security, Police Chief Van Benbow deputized thirty Munsonians to assist "the regular force in suppressing all forms of rowdyism and crime."[390]

Headline from the *Muncie Morning Star*, October 30, 1906. *Scanned from microfilm at Ball State University's Bracken Library.*

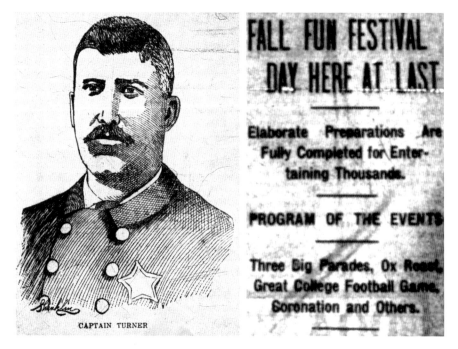

Above, left: MPD captain Curtis Turner, from the *Muncie Morning Star*, September 8, 1899. *Scanned from microfilm at Ball State University's Bracken Library.*

Above, right: Headline from the *Muncie Morning Star*, October 31, 1906. *Scanned from microfilm at Ball State University's Bracken Library.*

Opposite: Halloween postcard, early 1900s. *Courtesy of the Wellcome Collection.*

The day before Halloween, former MPD officer Curtis Turner slaughtered six oxen for the barbecue. Boosters had leased an empty lot just south of the downtown post office to roast the beasts. Massive slabs of meat were "suspended on heavy steel rails" and slow cooked "over a big trench in true Kentucky style."[391]

When the day finally came, the "crisp air and bright sunshine caused thousands of people to appear upon the streets."[392] Union Traction reported that "every interurban car that entered the city was fairly packed to the roof with humanity and they are still coming."[393] The city's schools and most factories closed for the day.

Festivities began with the Industrial Parade, which featured dozens of elaborately decorated floats "by businessmen and manufacturers…forming a most attractive pageant."[394] At the end sat the King of Enterprise, mounted in a handsome wagon. The parade snaked through downtown and ended

at the Court of Honor on High Street, which stretched between Main and Adams. Especially paved for the event, the court also served as the dance floor for the night's ball.

The crowd rushed to the barbecue after. The "fat and juicy oxen had been roasted in pits" and served to the crowd "between the covers of delicious buns."[395] The meat quickly ran out. One of the cooks told a

Young Munsonians all dressed for Halloween in 1916. *Courtesy of Ball State University Libraries' Bracken Archive and Special Collections.*

reporter that he didn't think "there were enough people in Muncie to eat six oxen in two hours."[396]

The Floral Parade began promptly at a half past one. The procession featured a legion of automobiles and horse carriages decked out in flowers.

The Queen of Halloween herself rode in a car draped in chrysanthemums. When the parade was over, "there was a grand rush to board street cars for Southside Park" at the corner of Second and Walnut. "After a herculean struggle," Rose Polytechnic beat DePauw 10–9 in front of 2,500 spectators.[397]

As the sun sank into the horizon, about five hundred masked revelers led the King and Queen in the Parade of the Masqued Courtiers. The Queen of Halloween was officially crowned, as was her consort, revealed now to be Roy Munson Friedley. Munsonians then danced the night away under a brilliantly lit arch of "hundreds of colored electric lights." Thousands packed downtown, and "merriment reigned supreme till a late hour, when the streets resumed their wonton nocturnal quietude."[398]

Vaudeville actor Erroll Dunbar, pre-1890. Dunbar performed at the Star Theater. *Courtesy of the Delaware County Historical Society*, Star Theater Collection.

Masquerade balls, house parties and parades came and went over the next twenty years. The street festivals did, too, although they never rivaled the scale found on Muncie's gas boom Halloweens. The pranks and mischief continued well into the 1950s.

But just over a century ago, the Magic City on All Hallows' Eve transformed at night "into a veritable fairyland, crowded with merrymakers grotesquely costumed."[399]

CHAPTER 13

THE HAUNTING OF OLD TOWN HILL

O f all the ghost stories that appear in Delaware County's historical record, the July 1867 haunting of Old Town Hill is the one told most often. The exact details of what happened that summer are murky, as no Muncie newspaper from 1867 has survived. It is, however, certain that a haunting of some kind occurred, as two contemporary diarists wrote entries noting the spectacle as it happened. A hardware wholesaler and politician in Muncie named Frederick Putnam mentioned it in his journal on Thursday, July 25, 1867:

> *Warm and sultry in morning, a good rain in P.M. Presbyterian and Methodist Sabbath School Picnic at Chesterfield today—Great excitement on Ghost question at Sam Cecil's or Old Town. Trade very fair.*[400]

Thomas Neely, a Munsonian blacksmith at the time, wrote in his diary a day later:

> *A number of persons, last evening, went up to old town hill to see some kind of fiery apparition that had been witnessed by some person the night before. But there was nothing supernatural to be seen.*[401]

The earliest surviving local version of the full story dates to an 1880 *Muncie Daily Times* article titled "Twice-Told Tale."[402] The story began in the summer of 1867 when a "party of treasure-hunters" went digging in the "range of hills located in the southeastern part of this [Centre] Township."[403] In the early and mid-nineteenth century, this hilly area along the White River southeast of Muncie was known as Old Town Hill. The treasure-hunters were searching for "a vast deal of gold and silver coin," supposedly left by "a powerful and wealthy tribe of Indians."[404]

The diggers learned of the treasure from "the lips of an old Indian who was living with Mr. Borter Rees." Although the 1880 story doesn't give the Native person's name, the source was likely a reference to James Musco. If you'll recall from the end of the tenth chapter, Musco remained along the White River with his family after the Lenape left Indiana in 1820. He later lived on the Rees farm about a mile and a half southeast of Old Town Hill in Perry Township.

One balmy July 1867 evening, "as the shades of eventide were setting down upon the scene," the treasure-hunters digging on Old Town Hill were interrupted by a low roar emanating from the wetland below the hill. The noise "grated on their ears in a most bewitchingly peculiar, strange and frightful manner."[405]

The diggers dropped their shovels to scan the swamp and woody hillside for the

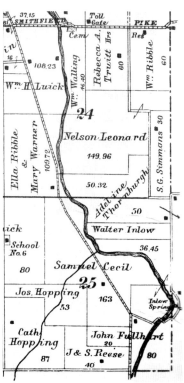

Top: James Musco's tombstone at Rees Cemetery. *Photo taken by the author.*

Bottom: Old Town Hill is where the pike, creek and river meet on Sam Cecil's farm. Image taken from the 1887 *Atlas of Delaware County. Courtesy of the Delaware County Historical Society.*

source of the terrible sound. One of them spotted a brilliant luminescence a short distance away. "As the light came toward them, they quaked in their boots. The strange inanimate light, which looked like a jack-o'-lantern, came up from the swamp, which was known to be impassable by any living being."[406]

The men grew terrified yet were strangely transfixed as the brightness drew near. Suddenly, "a stream of betwitching light, which blinded them all, poured from the monstrous being and was bearing down on them, and fearing that they would be swallowed up like Jonah was by the whale, they flew from the scene."

News of the haunting, or whatever it was, spread quickly across Muncie and east-central Indiana. People flocked nightly to Old Town Hill for a glimpse of the ghost. Come evening, New Burlington Pike southeast of the city "was jammed with buggies, carriages and horsemen."[407] Southside livery stables inflated the price to rent rigs each evening—"every boneyard in the bailiwick was at fancy prices." Some were unwilling to pay the exorbitant fees and went out to Old Town Hill on foot. It was only four miles southeast of the city.

Three nights later, "the largest party of men assembled on Old Town Hill that had ever before or after congregated at one place in the county."[408] Everyone, it seemed, wanted a glimpse of the ghost.

A hush fell over the crowd not long after sunset. The darkness was broken abruptly by a light coming up from the swamp "like some enchanting devil, it arose from the centre of the quagmire, and started toward the crowd." Some ran, others screamed. A group of "old frontiersmen who had fought Indians and lived on venison for a score of years…who feared nothing" moved toward the ghost to see "what there was in the hallucination."

But then, a "ray of peculiar light began to radiate in their furrowed faces." These aging settlers, perhaps fearing death as one frontier too far, stepped back in terror, "affected by the influence of some mysterious power, they knew not what." When they realized that the ghosts were coming for them, "they fled to their horses and vehicles and broke for home."[409]

Many more spectators came the following night, even from as far away as Cincinnati. As swarms of people gathered on the hill, all manner of speakers gave addresses about the phenomenon. Those who ran the previous night "were denounced by some as cowards." Others tried to rationalize the haunting with pseudoscientific nonsense. A young doctor Kemper from Muncie delivered a loony speech "in which he said he could not understand why the ghosts and different kinds of lights were appearing in the dark at Old Town Hill unless it was the phosphorus from the body coming up through the ground from the dead Indians buried there, forming into different strange lights and forms."[410]

The crowd on this fourth night also had a particularly rowdy component to it—armed men with something to prove. They "formed into companies and, with pistols in hand, said they would face the monster."

Then without notice, "the evil one appeared" and came up from the swamp:[411]

There was a clicking of pistol-locks, a clenching of teeth, and a vowing that "we stand shoulder to shoulder." When the light came near enough to enable those who were armed to do effective pistol work, a strange feeling came over them (those who had so loudly talked), and they feared to shoot lest they insulted their Deity, and they ran like sheep![412]

The 1880 story in the *Muncie Daily Times* concluded by noting that the crowds continued for about a week and then dissipated. The ghosts of Old Town Hill were never seen again.

Different versions of this story appeared frequently in Muncie newspapers in the late nineteenth and early twentieth centuries. The tale was even recorded by Works Progress Administration (WPA) workers as late as 1937.[413] The various tellings emphasize different aspects, and some details changed over time. By the mid-twentieth century, the story of Old Town Hill's 1867 haunting had passed into folklore. This makes it difficult to separate out historical fact from legend.

However, there are some indisputable certainties to this tale, such as the name Old Town Hill. When Americans first colonized what we now call Delaware County in the 1820s to 1830s, settlers referred to the series of bluffs along the White River southeast of Munseytown as "Old Town Hill." The name was likely a reference to the Lenape village of Wapikamicoke that had once existed on the hill from 1796 until about 1812. Today, the village site is near the intersection of Burlington Drive and Inlow Springs Road.

After the Northwest Indian War formally ended with the Treaty of Greenville in 1795, the main band of Lenape resettled on ancestral Myaamia (Miami) land in what the Americans called the Northwest Territory. The Lenape established about a dozen villages along the West Fork of the White River. The first was Wapikamicoke, followed by Munseytown and then Owenachki. All three were in what is now Delaware County. Several other villages existed downriver, including Killbuck's Village and Wapiminisink— chief Kikthawenund's village (present-day Anderson).

Smithfield Pike/Inlow Springs Road in the 1890s. *Courtesy of Ball State University Libraries' Bracken Archive and Special Collections.*

Wapikamicoke was home to Lenape chief Buckongahelas and about forty families. A revered military commander and effective leader, Buckongahelas was an instrumental tribal elder in the late 1700s. With other chiefs, he led many Lenape west as Americans colonized Native lands beyond the Appalachian Mountains. Buckongahelas was an old man by the time he lived along the White River from 1796 until his death from smallpox in 1805.

The village slowly depopulated afterward. During the War of 1812, Wapikamicoke was abandoned altogether. During the conflict, tribal elders attempted to keep White River Lenape neutral as noncombatants. They even temporarily moved to Piqua, Ohio, at the behest of Indiana's territorial government.

Sometime in late spring of 1813, the now abandoned Wapikamicoke and Munseytown villages were burned to the ground. The Lenape returned to the White River after the war, but most relocated downriver to Wapiminisink (Anderson's Village), Little Munsee Town, Conner's Village and Brouette's Village. Wapikamicoke was thereafter called "Old Town" and then later "Old Town Hill" as a nod to the abandoned Native settlement.

Wapikamicoke also sat on an ancient thoroughfare connecting Native towns along the Whitewater River to those on the Wabash, by way of the White River watershed in what is now Delaware County. The trace connected Wapikamicoke to Munseytown and the Myaamia villages on the

Wabash. The state built the Richmond and Logansport Road over much of this trail in the 1830s. For many years thereafter, settlers referred to this rough corduroy highway as 'Richmond Road.'

Not long after the Civil War in 1867, the same year as the haunting, some of this road southeast of Muncie became part of the Muncie and New Burlington Turnpike. The new gravel bed made it easy for Munsonians to travel out to Old Town Hill and nearby Inlow Springs—a popular picnic spot near the hill.

The Lenape and Myaamiaki were coerced into treaties with the U.S. government in 1818 to relinquish all land in central Indiana. The White River Lenape had until 1821 to leave the state, although most left for Missouri in 1820. The feds then sold the stolen Native land to mostly white farmers at rock-bottom prices with favorable terms of credit.

The Cecil families were some of the first settlers to colonize the area, eventually fanning out and buying tracts in Liberty, Center and Perry Townships. Samuel I. Cecil of Virginia bought most of Old Town Hill—153 acres of bluffs, forests, swamps and farmland. At some point, he sold or gave the property to his brother Aaron Cecil. Aaron and his wife, Anna, had settled in 1831 nearby in Perry Township. The Cecils had seven children, including a son Sam, so named in honor of his uncle.[414]

Little Sam Cecil grew up and married Rhoda Truitt in 1847. The couple settled on Old Town Hill, after Sam purchased the soil-rich property from his father. He then spent the next half century farming it. He retired to Muncie around 1900 and died at the age of ninety-two in 1916.

True or not, many of the legends surrounding Old Town Hill come from Sam Cecil. In his obit, the *Muncie Morning Star* wrote that "Mr. Cecil remembered many stories of the Indians and took great delight in telling the numerous queer habits and superstitions of the early settlers."[415]

In one story, Cecil described Wapikamicoke's remains as covering two acres at the hill's summit:

> *The village stood on an elevation of 100 feet above White river with a deep gully on the south-west, and sloping gently to the south eight rods to a creek called Juber, after an Indian chief. Beyond this creek forty rods stood an Indian trading post. Around this, several acres had been cleared and cultivated in corn.*[416]

In addition to the remains of a council house, Cecil claimed to have discovered an "Indian torture stake" at the same site. The wooden pole was

PIONEER OF MUNSEYTOWN AND HIS DESCENDANTS

Samuel Cecil Tells Many Interesting Stories of the Indians About Old Town Hill

Carl Cecil, 20.

Dr. A. A. Cecil, 50.   Samuel Cecil, 80.

William A. Cecil, 15 months.

Sam Cecil (*far right*) and family. *Muncie Morning Star*, February 5, 1904.

about seven to ten inches in diameter and stood to the side of Richmond Road at the hill's summit. At this very post, according to Cecil, the Lenape had burned to death a captured spy under command of American general Anthony Wayne. Cecil attributed this story to James Musco.[417] Another settler recalled that the stake "was of oak and was some ten feet high. At about the height of a tall man, the rough outline of a human face had been cut on each side."[418]

Thomas Neely remembered the same stake, recalling in 1881 that he came across it as a boy in 1839 when moving to Muncie. The wooden pole stood inclined on a:

piece of ground near the side of the then Richmond State Road, now the New Burlington Pike—where, tradition says, a Col. Winchester was burned at the stake by the Indians. The stake was visible when I came, and was charred; around it, for a distance of about fifty feet, it was level and smooth, and round like a circus ring…This tradition had gained considerable credence at the time, and all believed it to be true.[419]

Another settler named George Eddy recalled seeing the post later at the Delaware County Courthouse—"It was the same torture stake that I saw in the circle south of Muncie."[420] According to Cecil, during William Henry Harrison's 1840 presidential campaign, "The Whig party took the stake away and sent parts of it to every State in the Union as a token of respect to him as an Indian fighter."[421]

Cecil and the other settlers confused very real historical events and warped them into a legend explaining the wooden pole found on Old Town Hill. The post was never used to torture anyone, certainly not a "Colonel Winchester." Given the descriptions, it was likely the center support for the roof of a special longhouse used by Lenape during the Big House Ceremony. In the words of anthropologist Jay Miller, the Big House or Gamwing was an "integrative rite, expressing community identity and cosmic harmony from ancient times."[422] Half-red, half-black human faces known as M'sing were carved on either side of the center support pole to represent a spirit force.[423]

I couldn't find any historical record mentioning a Colonel Winchester being burned at the stake in Wapikamicoke. However, back in June 1782, Lenape warriors under the command of Captain Pipe captured and burned colonel William Crawford to death along the Sandusky River. Crawford, a close friend of George Washington's, was executed by Pipe's warriors in retaliation for the Gnadenhutten Massacre. Crawford's grisly end was a well-known war story told among farmers who settled the Northwest Territory. A real-life general, James Winchester had served in Revolutionary War and in the War of 1812. However, he died in 1826 at Gallatin, Tennessee.

Cecil's ghost tales of Old Town Hill were also poor attempts to incorporate the very real historical events of 1806.[424] A year before, a Munsee speaker named Beata had a series of visions warning the White River Lenape to re-embrace ancestral ways and abandon white people's culture, religion and alcohol. Her message was welcomed by many younger members of the tribe.

Beata's visions coincided with those of Tenskwatawa, the Shawnee prophet, who was living downriver in a village with his brother Tecumseh. Tenskwatawa was invited in 1806 by Munseytown Lenape to judge the "witches" among them—those who had crossed Beata's new tribal boundaries. Moravian missionaries living near what is now Anderson identified four killings in their diaries: Anne Charity (also named Caritas) and Joshua, two Native believers in Moravianism, along with Munseytown chief Tetepachsit and his nephew Billy Patterson. Charity was killed with lye, while Joshua and Patterson were burned alive, all at Munseytown. Tetepachsit was killed with a hatchet at the Moravian mission in what is now Anderson.[425]

It's hard to say how much of this history Sam Cecil knew when crafting his tale. Whatever the extent of his historical knowledge, it didn't limit him from incorporating new details into retellings of Old Town Hill's haunting. Cecil also liked to share a local legend that dated back to the 1820s regarding buried treasure, supposedly hidden by Lenape villagers before leaving during the War of 1812.

"People used to come from miles around to see the hill," Cecil told a reporter in 1900.[426] "Tales of hidden wealth were scattered everywhere. Every bit of this ground has been dug over by fortune hunters."[427] Cecil was certain that a hoard of coins lay "beneath the earth's surface in the way of kettles of gold secreted by the Indians years ago."[428]

Two treasure-hunters from Ohio once told Cecil that a U.S. spy named John Flinn supposedly learned about buried kettles full of gold or silver left behind at Wapikamicoke when the Lenape left in the War of 1812. According to Cecil, Flinn returned to the hill during the war and stole it. He absconded to "Ohio, where he spent his declining years in peace and plenty."[429] Cecil claimed that he himself had discovered a large copper kettle buried on his Old Town Hill farm in 1863, although it was empty.[430]

The story was tied together with a bit of supernatural string. There was, of course, a "mystic side to the legend of the buried treasure." The kettle was supposedly "guarded by the ghost of a big old Indian chief, and whenever the treasure was approached too closely by white men, he would appear and the air would be blue and hazy for a week."[431]

Cecil and other southeast Center Township farmers routinely caught and sometimes helped diggers search for treasure on the hill. One group from Wayne County in the 1840s brought a clairvoyant with them: "They had a medium in a trance at the Cecil home and at his direction, they dug at a certain designated spot." But not long after starting their dig, the treasure-hunters inexplicably became "seized with terror" and fled.[432]

In the 1850s, a group of gold diggers returning from the California Gold Rush stopped to dig at the hill. They deployed "mineral rods" to search for the kettle. If you're unfamiliar, a mineral rod is a special type of divining rod—a pseudoscientific "device" that guides an individual to something hidden like water, graves or buried treasure. The process of using such a rod is usually called dowsing, water witching or doodlebugging. Dowsing has the same efficacy as guessing. The *Muncie Morning Star* described the diggers' mineral rod as "an instrument which contains mercury and indicates the location of metal"—like a stash of coins.[433]

The diggers deployed it on Cecil's farm "one dark midnight" in summer. He reminisced to a reporter, "I was watching them dig. Suddenly a huge bolt of fire shot out from the woods and across the clearing toward us."[434] In another version of this story, Cecil said that the "California gold seekers" were "frightened away by the appearance of a shooting star that went over them."[435]

The story of buried gold and silver attracted diggers to Old Town Hill for decades. On a late July afternoon in 1867, two such men were in Muncie sharing a wild tale at the Mock Brick Yard near Five Points. According to those in attendance, the prospectors alleged an encounter with a ghost two nights before when digging on the hill.[436] A yard worker listening to the story interjected at the end, telling the crowd that he, too, had seen the ghost just the night before when fishing below the hill along the bank of the White River.[437]

The final confirmation of an Old Town Hill haunting came from a group of Munsonians picnicking one July evening nearby at Inlow Springs. Serving as an informal park, Inlow Springs was located southeast of Old Town Hill along Burlington Pike. On their way home, the picnickers "heard uncanny noises as they went by the hill and they saw mysterious lights in the hollow down by the river."[438]

These stories spread quickly across Muncie and the region in the hot summer of 1867, drawing crowds nightly to Old Town Hill. Visitors didn't know it at the time, but the haunting was an elaborate prank. The conspirators were Sam Cecil, brothers Jim and John Mock, George Parsons, George Gates, George Shaw, John Fullhart and Wess Trigo.[439] This motley crew of "ghosts" included recent Civil War vets Shaw, Trigo and Fullhart. The teenage Mock brothers and probably other area youngsters helped deploy the ghosts. The scheme was orchestrated by Old Town Hill farmers Cecil and Parsons, with an assist from George Gates, a Perry Township neighbor.

The reasons behind the elaborate ruse varied in the telling. In Cecil's early stories, he and his co-conspirators carried out the haunting to spook treasure-hunters away from digging up Old Town Hill. It backfired one night in July

Meeks Mortuary hearse crossing Inlow Springs near Old Town Hill, circa 1900. *Courtesy of Ball State University Libraries' Bracken Archive and Special Collections.*

1867 and drew even more people. Cecil and his "confederates executed the ghost stunt so cleverly that a couple of scientists had been summoned from Cincinnati to investigate the phenomenon."[440]

In another version of the tale, the ghosts were Cecil and Fullhart's reprisal against city folk picnicking at Inlow Springs. The farmers overheard Munsonians mocking the rural residents of Old Town Hill one evening and retaliated by "haunting" them on their way home.

There's probably some truth to this, as the newly built Muncie and New Burlington Turnpike provided easy access for city folk to visit Old Town Hill and Inlow Springs. The sudden and frequent influx of rowdy urbanites into tranquil rural Delaware County likely created friction—"the ghosts were created to get revenge on the city 'dudes.'"

In yet a third telling of the story, the haunting began as a trick played by the Mock brothers on their gullible friend Charlie Luick. The three worked together at the Mock Brick Yard with a few Civil War vets who had recently returned home. One day in July 1867, Luick overheard his coworkers share ghost stories about Old Town Hill.

Seeing his interest and knowing their over-trusting friend well, they convinced him to go digging for gold one night. Not long after he started, the

Stepping stones at Inlow Springs, circa 1900. *Courtesy of the Delaware County Historical Society, Mike Mavis Collection.*

The original ghost lantern from the Old Town Hill haunting (*right*), with the replica (*left*) in 1937. *Courtesy of Ball State University Libraries' Bracken Archive and Special Collections.*

vets, dressed as ghosts, made a frightful arrival. Poor Charlie Luick "made a lightning stampede to his grandmother's home, about a mile away."[441] They repeated the prank the next night on a fisherman, and then, "without announcement, there were more than 100 persons" arriving nightly on Old Town Hill.[442]

Whatever the original motivation, the Old Town Hill spirits of July '67 deployed a series of tactics to terrorize the gathering crowds. The team made different kinds of ghosts, "but the one that worked best was the stove pipe." Wess Trigo cut out a few dozen hideous faces from thin metal and fashioned them onto a hollow box with a torch inside. Then the "ghosts would appear down the river, from behind the trees and sometimes on the main road of Old Town Hill."[443]

These uncanny faces materialized in and out of shadows, scaring folks as they gathered. Just after sunset, George Shaw floated by on his canoe. He then sank "a jug into the river and blew into it," producing an unearthly howl. Shaw called his audible ghost "the roaring bull and everyone who heard it would be paralyzed with fear."[444]

Old Town Hill in 1954. *Courtesy of Ball State University Libraries' Bracken Archive and Special Collections.*

After this terrible roar, death like silence would seem to grip the throats of every living creature, then a light would appear to start out of the high tree and slowly make its way directly over the spot where the kettle had been found. This was done by pulling a lantern from one tree to another.[445]

Finally, after the roaring bull "had performed and the lantern made its appearance, a troupe of pale ghosts representing some of the departed Indians would come up from the river." The ghosts blinded the spectators by shining bright lights in their faces.

The haunting continued on and off for a few days. On the final night, about two thousand people covered Old Town Hill, and "many had rifles."[446] A conspirator spotted the guns after deploying a ghost face and went to warn his fellow phantoms. The pranksters abandoned the haunt then and there, leaving a lone ghost glowing on a pike.

Come morning, armed spectators surrounded the spectral head with their guns drawn. Alas, the breaking daylight revealed "only a smoking lantern and an old disfigured wooden shoe box." For several days, the ghost face "was exhibited in the old courthouse yard."[447]

John Mock later recalled that "it was a long time before the public knew the true story."[448]

EPILOGUE

I thought when I finished writing this book, I'd arrive at some profound new insight as to why so many old ghosts haunted Muncie. But there doesn't seem to be a through line. Some of our forebears saw spirits to explain phenomena they didn't understand. Others were haunted by memories of departed loved ones. A few even materialized ghosts to terrorize and exhilarate their neighbors. For many people living in the Gilded Age, stories of uncanny hauntings expressed the dark, unexplainable feelings that often linger after a traumatic experience.

The "modern" discourse about hauntings is overly concerned about proving or disproving whether ghosts exist. "Are ghosts real?" "What evidence is there of a haunting?" These are stupid questions. Ghosts are real for those who see and hear them. Plus, aren't we all just a little haunted by people we once knew, at least some of the time?

No one will ever "prove" that ghosts "exist" because they lie beyond the measure of human instruments. They haunt the liminal space between our senses and emotions, conjured from charged memories loitering at the edge of consciousness. Our conscience can summon them too, for ghosts appear anytime uncertainty comes crashing against a strong force of inexplicable emotion.

Death and Doctor Hornbook.

William Hole's rendering of the Robert Burns poem "Death and Doctor Hornbook."
Courtesy of Old Book Illustrations.

Notes

Introduction

1. "Opera House Is Haunted," *Muncie Morning Star*, March 31, 1900, 2.
2. "Heard Down the Line," *Muncie Daily Herald*, April 2, 1900, 8.

Chapter 1

3. "City News," *Muncie Daily News*, September 23, 1882, 1.
4. Ibid.
5. Charles Emerson, *Muncie City Directory*, 1881, 82.
6. "'Nat' Lockwood Is Dead at Frankfort," *Journal and Courier*, February 28, 1940, 3.
7. "City Items," *Muncie Daily News*, February 20, 1880, 1.
8. "Mysterious Marauders," *Muncie Daily News*, August 2, 1890, 3.
9. "No Ghost," *Muncie Daily News*, August 5, 1890, 3.
10. Ibid.
11. "Local News," *Muncie Daily Times*, May 23, 1893, 5.
12. "Montpelier," *Muncie Star*, September 5, 1934, 2; Find-A-Grave, "Ida L. Winget," https://www.findagrave.com/memorial/27183317/ida-l-winget.
13. "A White Spectre," *Muncie Daily Herald*, June 15, 1893, 3.
14. Ibid.
15. Ibid.

16. Ibid.
17. "Ghostly Noises Heard in Police Headquarters Lead Many to Believe," *Muncie Daily Herald*, December 19, 1893, 3.
18. Ibid.
19. "Suicide," *Muncie Daily Times*, October 8, 1890, 4.
20. "A Sad Story," *Muncie Daily Times*, October 9, 1890, 1.
21. "Smithfield Slivers," *Muncie Daily Herald*, November 25, 1897, 3.
22. "A Smithfield Ghost," *Muncie Daily Times*, August 19, 1899, 1.
23. "They See a Ghost," *Muncie Daily Times*, January 31, 1899, 1.
24. "Colored Boy Who Stole Wheels Was Ingenious," *Muncie Morning Star*, October 13, 1903, 5.
25. "Colored Lad Says Ghost Is in the County Jail," *Muncie Evening Times*, October 13, 1903, 1.
26. Ibid.
27. Ibid.
28. "Three State Cases," *Muncie Morning Star*, October 15, 1903, 3.
29. "Criminals Fear Supernatural," *Muncie Evening Times*, October 15, 1903, 1.
30. Ibid.
31. Ibid.
32. "Insane Man Was Shooting Up Home," *Muncie Evening Press*, November 20, 1907, 1.
33. Ibid.
34. Ibid.
35. "Carried Out Threats to Commit Suicide," *Muncie Morning Star*, March 5, 1907, 5.
36. Ibid.
37. Sarah Bricker and Mia Fields, "Using Leisure," in *The Other Side of Middletown* (Walnut Creek, CA: AltaMira Press, 2004), 159–60.
38. Ibid.
39. Keith Roysdon, "The Legend of Elliott Hall's Resident Ghost Lives On," *Muncie Evening Press*, October 27, 1986, 14.
40. Diane Goudy, "Elliott Hall Carries Legacy of Death," *Ball State Daily News*, January 16, 1986, 6.
41. Roysdon, "Legend of Elliott Hall's Resident Ghost," 14.
42. Popeguilty's story is set on the fifth floor of Bracken Library, but there are actually only four floors. See https://www.reddit.com/r/nosleep/comments/iz2km/why_i_wont_go_back.
43. Ibid. Italics in the original.
44. See https://thisisindiana.angelfire.com/indianahauntings.htm.

45. Ibid.
46. Douglas Walker, "Deputies: Man Caught Burglarizing High School," *Muncie Star Press*, April 28, 2020, 2.
47. Ibid.

Chapter 2

48. "Car Crew Startled by Woman in Black," *Muncie Star*, September 30, 1907, 1.
49. Ibid.
50. "Woman in Black Terrorizes Suburb," *Muncie Star*, June 7, 1907, 1.
51. Ibid.
52. Ibid.
53. "Masquerader Causing Concern in Industry," *Muncie Evening Press*, June 8, 1907, 8.
54. Ibid.
55. *Emerson's Muncie Directory, 1907, 1908*, Delaware County Historical Society, Heritage Collection.
56. Earl Conn, *Beneficence: Stories About the Ball Families of Muncie* (Muncie, IN: Minnetrista Cultural Foundation, 2003), 23.
57 "Woman in Black Terrorizes Suburb," 1.
58. "Suburb in Terror: Stranger at Large," *Muncie Star*, June 9, 1907, 1.
59. Ibid.
60. Ibid.
61. "Woman in Black Again Encountered," *Muncie Star*, June 18, 1907, 1.
62. Ibid.
63. "Practical Jokers in Serious Prank," *Muncie Star*, June 14, 1907, 1.
64. "Woman in Black Terrorizes Suburb," 1.
65. "Woman in Black Seen in Park," *Muncie Evening Press*, June 19, 1907, 8.
66. "Woman in Black Terrorizes Suburb," 1.
67. "Suburb in Terror," 1.
68. Ibid.
69. "Practical Jokers in Serious Prank," 1.
70. Ibid.
71. Ibid.
72. Ibid.
73. "Terror Is in Hiding," *Muncie Star*, June 27, 1907, 1.
74. "Practical Jokers in Serious Prank," 1.

75. Ibid.

76. "Woman in Black Out with a Gun," *Muncie Morning Star*, August 1, 1907, 1.

77. Ibid.

78. "The Woman in Black," *Muncie Star*, August 2, 1907, 10.

79. "Woman in Black Has Disappeared," *Muncie Evening Press*, September 14, 1907, 3.

80. "Woman in Black Again in Evidence," *Muncie Star*, September 23, 1907, 10.

81. Ibid.

82. Ibid.

83. "The Man in Black Is Now to Be Seen," *Muncie Evening Press*, October 12, 1907, 5.

84. "That Woman in Black," *Muncie Morning Star*, September 21, 1907, 1.

85. Ibid.

86. "Woman in Black Grabs Another Man," *Muncie Morning Star*, October 1, 1907, 1.

87. "Woman Scared Boys," *Muncie Star*, October 11, 1907, 16.

88. "Men Held in Spell by Woman in Black," *Muncie Star*, October 7, 1907, 1.

89. "Is Woman in Black Member of Black Hand?," *Muncie Evening Press*, October 3, 1907, 1.

90. "Knows Who 'She' Is," *Muncie Star*, October 2, 1907, 10.

91. Ibid.

92. "Halted by Black Form," *Muncie Star*, October 15, 1907, 10.

93. "Stayed Out All Night," *Muncie Star*, December 6, 1907, 16.

Chapter 3

94. "Every Seven Years," *Muncie Morning News*, August 14, 1892, 1.

95. Ibid.

96. Ibid.

97. Ibid.

98. Ibid.

99. Ibid.

100. Ibid.

101. Ibid.

102. See full text of the treaty at Ohio Memory, https://ohiomemory.org/digital/collection/p15005coll39/id/4550.

103. Thomas Helm, *History of Delaware County, Indiana Illustrated* (Chicago: Kingman Brothers, 1881), plate facing page 130.

104. Ibid.

105. Ibid.

106. *Muncie Morning News*, March 18, 1882, 1.

107. "The Ice Factory," *Muncie Morning News*, March 12, 1891, 1.

108. "New Water Well," *Muncie Morning Star*, July 2, 1902, 3.

109. June Mull, "Marble Slab Marks Grave of Munseetown's First White Female Child in Beech Grove," *Muncie Morning Star*, May 13, 1941, 12.

110. "Skeletons Found in Basement Here," *Muncie Evening Press*, March 15, 1948, 1.

111. "A White Specter," *Muncie Evening Press*, August 13, 1892, 1.

112. Ibid.

113. Ibid.

114. "A Sudden Death," *Muncie Daily Herald*, January 7, 1892, 2.

115. Ibid.

116. "Every Seven Years," 1.

Chapter 4

117. "House Said to Be 'Haunted,'" *Muncie Morning Star*, July 30, 1905, 4.

118. "Story of 'Ghosts' Keeps House Empty," *Muncie Morning Star*, June 25, 1905, 20.

119. Ibid.

120. Ibid.

121. Ibid.

122. Ibid.

123. Ibid.

124. Ibid.

125. Ibid.

126. "Carrying the Mail in Muncie in 1853," *Muncie Morning Star*, December 4, 1904, 27.

127. "Avondale," *Muncie Morning News*, October 25, 1889, 3.

128. "Story of 'Ghosts' Keeps House Empty," 20.

129. "Failed to Arrest the Spook," *Muncie Morning Star*, June 28, 1905, 6.

130. "Crowd Awaited Spook," *Muncie Morning Star*, July 31, 1905, 6.

131. Ibid.

132. Ibid.

133. Ibid.

134. Ibid.

135. "Latest Ghost Story Explained," *Muncie Morning Star*, August 14, 1905, 2.
136. Ibid.
137. Ibid.
138. Ibid.
139. Ibid.
140. "Southside Spook Is Gone," *Muncie Morning Star*, November 22, 1905, 10.
141. Ibid.
142. Ibid.
143. Ibid.

Chapter 5

144. Roger Hensley, "The Central Indiana Railway," April 21, 2004, Railroads of Madison County. Available online at http://madisonrails. railfan.net/cirwy.html.
145. "Ghostly," *Muncie Daily Times*, February 22, 1896, 1.
146. Ibid.
147. Ibid.
148. Ibid.
149. Ibid.
150. Ibid.
151. Ibid.
152. Ibid.
153. Ibid.
154. "A Probable Murder," *Muncie Daily Times*, April 1, 1895, 1.
155. Ibid.
156. "Bright Is Dead," *Muncie Morning News*, April 2, 1895, 5.
157. "Probable Murder," 1.
158. Ibid.
159. "Simply Accidental," *Muncie Daily Times*, April 2, 1895, 1.
160. "Was It Murder?," *Muncie Daily Times*, April 6, 1895, 1.
161. Ibid.
162. "The Ghost," *Muncie Daily Times*, February 29, 1896, 1.
163. Ibid.
164. Ibid.
165. Ibid.
166. Ibid.
167. Ibid.

168. "It's a Horrid Fake," *Muncie Daily Times*, March 7, 1896, 4.
169. "That Horrible Ghost," *Muncie Daily Herald*, March 16, 1896, 8.

Chapter 6

170. Helm, *History of Delaware County, Indiana*, 52.
171. "Landers Ghost on the Pike," *Muncie Daily Herald*, July 23, 1896, 1.
172. Ibid.
173. "Foul Murder," *Muncie Daily Herald*, July 8, 1896, 1.
174. "Another Murder," *Muncie Daily Times*, July 8, 1896, 1.
175. "Murder Mystery," *Muncie Morning News*, July 9, 1896, 1.
176. "Foul Murder," 1.
177. Ibid.
178. "Murder Mystery," 1.
179. "Foul Murder," 1.
180. "Murder Mystery," 1.
181. Ibid.
182. Ibid.
183. Ibid.
184. Ibid.
185. "Still a Mystery," *Muncie Daily Times*, July 9, 1896, 1.
186. "Dark Mystery the Murder," *Muncie Daily Herald*, July 9, 1896, 1.
187. Ibid.
188. "Foul Murder," 1.
189. "Thomas Morgan Claimed by Death," *Muncie Morning Star*, November 19, 1911, 12.
190. Charles Emerson, *Muncie City Directory, 1893–1894* (Richmond, IN), 418.
191. "Joe Made Bogus Money," *Muncie Daily Herald*, March 3, 1897, 1.
192. "Murder Mystery," 1.
193. "Still a Mystery," 1.
194. "Murder Mystery," 1.
195. Ibid.
196. Ibid.
197. Ibid.
198. "Landers Not Murdered," *Muncie Daily Herald*, July 10, 1896, 1.
199. "Lander's Ghost on the Pike," *Muncie Daily Herald*, July 23, 1896, 1.

Chapter 7

200. "The Headless Horseman," *Indianapolis News*, November 2, 1901, 3.

201. Ibid.

202. Ibid.

203. Ibid.

204. Ibid.

205. Ibid.

206. See Ted Shideler's Schoolhousery website, https://schoolhousery.net/delaware-county/delaware-county-salem-township.

207. Dick Greene, "Seen and Heard in Our Neighborhood," *Muncie Star*, September 18, 1954, 6.

208. I think this was a typo in the paper and they meant, "Legend of an Indian Treasure."

209. Beth McCord, "The Ghosts of the Delaware: An Archaeological Study of Delaware Settlement Along the White River, Indiana," *Reports of Investigation* 62 (May 2002): 35. Ball State University, Archaeological Resources Management Service. Available at https://www.bsu.edu/-/media/www/departmentalcontent/aal/aalpdfs/roi-51-75/roi-62-public.pdf.

210. The 1809 Treaty of Fort Wayne suggested that he was still alive in that year. See https://americanindian.si.edu/static/nationtonation/pdf/Treaty-of-Fort-Wayne, 1809.pdf.

211. McCord, "Ghosts of the Delaware," 35.

212. Lenape Talking Dictionary, "fox," https://www.talk-lenape.org/results?query=fox.

213. English-Munsee Dictionary, "fox," https://glosbe.com/en/umu/fox.

214. Miami-Illinois Indigenous Language Digital Archive, https://mc.miamioh.edu/ilda-myaamia/dictionary/entries/3598.

215. "Headless Horseman," 3.

216. Ibid.

217. Ibid.

218. "Oliver Slack Dies at Home in Florida," *Muncie Star*, August 14, 1932, 17.

219. See the 1861 Mount Pleasant Township plat map, available at Ball State University Libraries' Bracken Archive and Special Collections and online at https://dmr.bsu.edu/digital/collection/HistMaps/id/297/rec/59.

220. "Yorktown Notes," *Muncie Morning News*, December 28, 1881, 2.

221. "Yorktown," *Muncie Daily Times*, May 22, 1880, 1.

222. "Whiskey at Fault," *Muncie Morning News*, August 23, 1883, 3.

223. Ibid.
224. Ibid.
225. Ibid.
226. *Indianapolis Journal,* January 11, 1886, 1.
227. *Huntington Democrat,* January 14, 1886, 3.
228. "Still Another Suicide," *Muncie Daily Times,* April 28, 1900, 1.
229. "Case that Caused a Suicide," *Muncie Daily Times,* May 17, 1900, 1.
230. "Drank Acid to End Life," *Muncie Morning Star,* April 29, 1900, 5.
231. "Released," *Muncie Morning News,* September 14, 1898, 5.
232. Ibid.
233. "Many Cases for Coroner," *Muncie Morning Star,* May 24, 1900, 6.
234. "Seeking Eternal Rest," *Muncie Daily Herald,* April 23, 1900, 1.
235. "Two Bullets in Brain," *Muncie Daily Times,* July 26, 1900, 1.
236. Ibid.
237. "A Puzzler for Physicians," *Muncie Daily Times,* August 2, 1900, 1.
238. "Shot Himself Five Times," *Muncie Morning Star,* August 7, 1900, 6.
239. "Headless Horseman," 3.
240. Ibid.
241. Ibid.
242. Ibid.
243. Ibid.
244. Ibid.
245. "Five Dollars for Spending the Night in Haunted House," *Indianapolis News,* November 11, 1901, 2.
246. "Charles Burgess Dies at Hospital," *Muncie Evening Press,* March 27, 1963, 24.

Chapter 8

247. "Arguments in Suit of County Submitted," *Muncie Evening Press,* May 23, 1924, 12.
248. "Viaduct Ghost East of City Is Drawing Crowds Nightly," *Muncie Morning Star,* April 12, 1930, 2.
249. Ibid.
250. Ibid.
251. *Muncie Evening Press,* April 12, 1930, 9.
252. "In the Press of Things," *Muncie Evening Press,* April 12, 1930, 4.
253. Ibid.

254. "Ghost Again Fails to Make Appearance," *Muncie Morning Star*, April 14, 1930, 12.

255. Ibid.

256. Ibid.

257. "In The Press of Things," *Muncie Evening Press*, April 15, 1930, 4.

258. Ibid.

259. "Still After Ghost," *Muncie Morning Star*, April 29, 1930, 12.

260. Dick Greene, "Seen and Heard in Our Neighborhood," *Muncie Star*, July 11, 1950, 6.

261. Dick Greene, "Seen and Heard in Our Neighborhood," *Muncie Star*, August 9, 1950, 6.

262. Ibid.

263. Ibid.

264. Ibid.

265. Ibid.

266. Ibid.

267. Ibid.

Chapter 9

268. "Air Raid Warning Test Tomorrow Afternoon," *Muncie Star*, September 7, 1942, 20.

269. "Plan State Air Raid Warning System," *Muncie Star*, September 18, 1941, 11.

270. "Air Raid Warning Test Monday Noon," *Muncie Star*, November 21, 1942, 3.

271. "Muncie Lights Turned Low in First Wartime Dim-Out," *Muncie Star*, November 30, 1942, 1.

272. Ibid.

273. Ibid.

274. "Defense Leaders Map Out Procedure for Black-Out," *Muncie Morning Star*, December 29, 1942, 1.

275. "Florence Bly Is Found Dead Outside Hotel," *Muncie Morning Star*, January 4, 1943, 1.

276. Ibid.

277. Ibid.

278. Ibid.

279. Ibid.

280. Ibid.

281. Ibid.

282. *Muncie Morning Star*, December 12, 1942, 10.

283. "Library to Close," *Muncie Evening Press*, January 5, 1943, 1.

284. Frederick Graham, *Radisson Hotel Roberts: Muncie's Historic Treasure*, 1997, 9. Booklet available at Ball State University's Bracken Archives and Special Collections.

285. Ibid.

286. Tom Baker and Jonathan Tichena, *Haunted Indianapolis and Other Indiana Ghost Stories* (Atglen, PA: Schiffer Publications, 2008), 82.

287. "Three Are Injured in Auto Collision," *Muncie Morning Star*, March 16, 1916, 16.

288. "Prizes Awarded Garden Plots," *Muncie Evening Press*, July 9, 1918, 13.

289. *Muncie Morning Star*, April 7, 1917.

290. "Society," *Muncie Evening Press*, April 24, 1925, 7.

291. *Muncie Evening Press*, February 27, 1925.

292. "Amos Whiteley Will Probated," *Muncie Star*, August 9, 1925, 21.

293. "Muncie Girls to Get Diplomas at Earlham," *Muncie Star*, June 8, 1930, 17.

294. "Lincoln School Branch Library Is City's Need," *Muncie Star*, February 11, 1931, 1.

295. "Librarian Is Given Two Months Leave," *Muncie Evening Press*, June 17, 1931, 2.

296. "Florence Bly Heads Maring Library," *Muncie Evening Press*, July 11, 1933, 2.

297. Ruth Mauzy, "Society News," *Muncie Evening Press*, April 11, 1935, 8.

298. "Social and Other Items of Interest," *Muncie Star*, April 13, 1936, 5.

299. "Grade School Roles Totaled," *Muncie Star*, September 10, 1940, 3.

300. "Garfield School Notes," *Muncie Star*, March 15, 1941, 2.

301. "Story Hour at Branch," *Muncie Star*, December 22, 1942, 10.

302. Florence Bly's death certificate, Indiana Archives and Records Administration. Document is available courtesy of Ancestry.com.

Chapter 10

303. John Gibson, "The Ghost of the Headless Tinware Peddler," *Muncie Evening Press*, March 14, 1936, 6.

304. Ibid.

305. Ibid.

306. Ibid.
307. Ibid.
308. Ibid.
309. Ibid.
310. Ibid.
311. Ibid.
312. Ibid.
313. Ibid.
314. John Will Gibson, "The White Dog," *Muncie Evening Press*, March 21, 1936, 5.
315. Ibid.
316. Ibid.
317. Ibid.
318. Ibid.
319. Ibid.
320. Ibid.
321. Ibid.
322. Ibid.
323. Ibid.
324. John Will Gibson, "The White-Robed Ghost of Rees's Graveyard," *Muncie Evening Press*, March 28, 1936, 6.
325. Ibid.
326. Ibid.
327. Ibid.
328. Ibid.
329. Ibid.

Chapter 11

330. See Indiana Department of Natural Resources, https://www.in.gov/dnr/historic-preservation/help-for-owners/national-and-state-registers/shaard-database.
331. Find-A-Grave, https://www.findagrave.com.
332. Helm, *History of Delaware County, Indiana*, 36.
333. John Carlson, "A Look into Local Cemetery Hauntings," *Star Press*, October 26, 2008, 43.
334. Ibid.
335. "A Spook Story," *Muncie Morning News*, September 30, 1879, 1.

336. Ibid.
337. Ibid.
338. Ibid.
339. "A Haunted Stable," *Muncie Daily Herald*, January 9, 1893, 3.
340. Ibid.
341. Ibid.
342. Ibid.
343. Ibid.
344. "Married," *Muncie Daily Times*, April 7, 1888, 1.
345. "Sensation at Cowan," *Muncie Daily Times*, July 23, 1894, 1.
346. "Obituary," *Muncie Daily Times*, July 28, 1894, 4.
347. "Proved Successful," *Muncie Daily Times*, July 26, 1894, 1.
348. "The Cowan Ghost," *Muncie Morning News*, July 17, 1895, 5.
349. Ibid.
350. Ibid.

Chapter 12

351. Lesley Pratt Bannatyne, *Halloween* (Gretna, LA: Pelican Publishing, 1990), 2.
352. "The Boys and Girls Were Gay," *Muncie Morning News*, November 1, 1889, 3.
353. "Hallow-een," *Muncie Morning News*, November 1, 1881, 4.
354. Ibid.
355. Ibid.
356. Ibid.
357. "Merry Masquers," *Muncie Morning News*, November 1, 1893, 1.
358. "False Faces," *Muncie Morning News*, November 1894, 1.
359. Ibid.
360. "Earthquake," *Muncie Morning News*, November 1, 1895, 8.
361. "Earthquake Shock," *Muncie Daily Times*, October 31, 1895, 1.
362. "Everybody Had Fun," *Muncie Daily Times*, October 31, 1895, 1.
363. "All Halloween," *Muncie Morning News*, November 1, 1895, 1.
364. "Wet to the Skin," *Muncie Morning News*, November 2, 1897, 1.
365. "A Time of Gayety," *Muncie Evening Press*, November 1, 1898, 2.
366. "Merry Making," *Muncie Morning News*, November 1, 1898, 5.
367. Ibid.
368. "Hallowe'en," *Muncie Morning News*, November 1, 1899, 5.

369. "Colored Maskers," *Muncie Morning News*, November 1, 1898, 5.

370. Ibid.

371. "Merry Making," 5.

372. Ibid.

373. "Ghosts Walked by Night," *Muncie Daily Times*, November 1, 1900, 1.

374. Ibid.

375. Ibid.

376. "Halloween Is Centuries Old; Wonderful Change in Celebration," *Muncie Morning Star*, November 1, 1900, 5.

377. Ibid.

378. "Revelry Sustained," *Muncie Evening Press*, November 1, 1900, 5.

379. "Night of Revelry on Muncie Streets," *Muncie Evening Press*, October 31, 1902, 1.

380. Ibid.

381. Ibid.

382. Another version of this section about the 1906 Fall Fun Festival was written originally as part of my "ByGone Muncie" column in the *Star Press*. The original version was published on October 29, 2021, and was titled "City Went Big for Celebration of All Hallow's Eve in 1906."

383. "Fall Fun Festival Launched Last Night," *Muncie Morning Star*, October 4, 1906, 6.

384. "Plans for Festival Are Very Elaborate," *Muncie Morning Star*, October 12, 1906, 3.

385. "Big Crowd Coming for Fall Festival," *Muncie Morning Star*, October 27, 1906, 3.

386. "Splendid Program for Fall Festival," *Muncie Morning Star*, October 22, 1906, 10.

387. Ibid.

388. "Big College Game in Muncie Wednesday," *Muncie Morning Star*, October 28, 1906, 4.

389. "Fall Fun Festival Launched Last Night," 6.

390. "Boosts Festival in Proclamation," *Muncie Morning Star*, October 28, 1906, 2.

391. "Thousands Enjoyed Fall Fun Festival," *Muncie Morning Star*, November 1, 1906, 1.

392. "Fall Festival in Muncie Starts Out Most Favorably," *Muncie Evening Press*, October 31, 1906, 1.

393. Ibid.

394. "Thousands Enjoyed Fall Fun Festival," 1.

395. Ibid.

396. Ibid.

397. Ibid.

398. Ibid.

399. "'Tis the Time of Ghosts," *Muncie Morning Star*, October 31, 1905, 6.

Chapter 13

400. Frederick Putnam Diaries, Ball State University Libraries' Bracken Archive and Special Collections. Available at https://dmr.bsu.edu/digital/collection/PtnmFrdDiar/id/3005/rec/8.

401. Thomas Neely Diaries, Ball State University Libraries' Bracken Archive and Special Collections. Available at https://dmr.bsu.edu/digital/collection/NlyThmsDiar/id/483/rec/1.

402. "Twice-Told Tale," *Muncie Daily Times*, January 12, 1880, 4. The *Times* noted in the introduction that the *Cincinnati Commercial* first published the version a week before.

403. Ibid. The article dates the story to summer of 1868, but as the contemporary diaries show, it was 1867.

404. Ibid.

405. Ibid.

406. Ibid.

407. Ibid.

408. Ibid.

409. Ibid.

410. Carrie Jordan, "The Ghosts of Old Town Hill," *Muncie Star*, September 25, 1927, 64.

411. Ibid.

412. Ibid. Parentheses are in the original.

413. Hurley Goodall, *A Comprehensive Look at the People and History of Delaware County, Indiana* (Muncie, IN: Ball State University Libraries, 1999). Goodall compiled this book from 1930s WPA interviews with county residents.

414. "County Pioneer Answers Call," *Muncie Morning Star*, January 17, 1916, 7.

415. Ibid.

416. "Indian Torture Post in Delaware County," *Indiana Quarterly Magazine of History* (Fourth Quarter 1905): 176–79. Juber Creek today is known as "Elwood Rees #203 Ditch."

417. Ibid.

418. William Smith, *Indiana Miscellany* (Cincinnati, OH: Poe and Hitchcock, 1867), 31.

419. Helm, *History of Delaware County, Indiana*, 38.

420. "Indian Torture Post in Delaware County," 176–79.

421. Ibid.

422. Jay Miller, "Old Religion Among the Delawares: The Gamwing (Big House Rite)," *Ethnohistory* 44, no. 1 (1997).

423. Frank Speck, *A Study of the Delaware Indian Big House Ceremony*, vol. 2 (Harrisburg: Pennsylvania Historical Commission, 1931), 35–36.

424. Jay Miller, "The 1806 Purge Among the Indiana Delaware," *Ethnohistory* 41, no. 2 (1994).

425. See Lawrence Gibson, *The Moravian Indian Mission on White River* (Indianapolis: Indiana Historical Bureau, 1938).

426. "The Old Indian Torture Stake," *Muncie Morning Star*, July 24, 1900, 6.

427. Ibid.

428. "Two Men After Treasure," *Muncie Daily Herald*, April 5, 1897, 1.

429. "Unveiling of Old Town Hill Marker," *Muncie Star*, June 13, 1915, 14.

430. After disappearing for many years, the kettle turned up in an attic in 1956. Evan Owens, "In the Press of Things," *Muncie Evening Press*, June 21, 1956, 4.

431. "Topics of the Town," *Muncie Morning News*, August 15, 1894, 4.

432. Ibid.

433. "Old Indian Torture Stake," 6.

434. Ibid.

435. "Unveiling the Old Town Hill Marker," *Muncie Star*, June 13, 1915, 14.

436. John Lewellen, "Gold-Diggers at Old Town Hill Scared by Ghost," *Muncie Evening Press*, May 8, 1937, 16.

437. "County Had a Ghost Scare," *Muncie Evening Press*, September 21, 1927, 2.

438. "Unveiling of Old Town Hill Marker," 14.

439. "County Had a Ghost Scare," 2.

440. "Still Active Man Though Nearly Ninety Years Old," *Muncie Evening Press*, July 21, 1911, 4.

441. Lewellen, "Gold-Diggers at Old Town Hill," 16.

442. Ibid.

443. "County Had a Ghost Scare," 2.

444. Ibid.

445. Ibid.

446. "County Had a Ghost Scare," 2.

447. "The Famous Ghost of 1865 and How It Was Exposed," *Muncie Morning Star*, May 22, 1904, 12.

448. "County Had a Ghost Scare," 2.

ABOUT THE AUTHOR

C hris Flook is a public historian from Muncie, Indiana, and has authored three books about local history in addition to *Ghosts of Old Muncie*: *Indianapolis Graverobbing*, *Native Americans of East-Central Indiana* and *Lost Towns of Delaware County*. In 2016, he coauthored and edited *Beech Grove Cemetery Comes to Life*. Flook also writes the bi-monthly "ByGone Muncie History" column for the *Star Press*. In addition to volunteering at the Delaware County Historical Society, Flook works professionally as a motion graphics designer, photographer and documentary filmmaker. He teaches motion design in the Department of Media at Ball State University as a senior lecturer.

FREE eBOOK OFFER

Scan the QR code below, enter your e-mail address and get our original Haunted America compilation eBook delivered straight to your inbox for free.

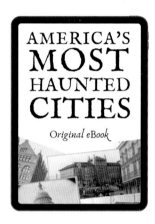

ABOUT THE BOOK

Every city, town, parish, community and school has their own paranormal history. Whether they are spirits caught in the Bardo, ancestors checking on their descendants, restless souls sending a message or simply spectral troublemakers, ghosts have been part of the human tradition from the beginning of time.

In this book, we feature a collection of stories from five of America's most haunted cities: Baltimore, Chicago, Galveston, New Orleans and Washington, D.C.

SCAN TO GET
AMERICA'S MOST HAUNTED CITIES

Having trouble scanning? Go to:
biz.arcadiapublishing.com/americas-most-haunted-cities